2021
Law of Attraction Planner

This Planner Belongs to:

2020 Calendar

January

M	T	W	T	F	S	S
		1	2	3	4	5
6	7	8	9	10	11	12
13	14	15	16	17	18	19
20	21	22	23	24	25	26
27	28	29	30	31		

February

M	T	W	T	F	S	S
					1	2
3	4	5	6	7	8	9
10	11	12	13	14	15	16
17	18	19	20	21	22	23
24	25	26	27	28	29	

March

M	T	W	T	F	S	S
						1
2	3	4	5	6	7	8
9	10	11	12	13	14	15
16	17	18	19	20	21	22
23	24	25	26	27	28	29
30	31					

April

M	T	W	T	F	S	S
		1	2	3	4	5
6	7	8	9	10	11	12
13	14	15	16	17	18	19
20	21	22	23	24	25	26
27	28	29	30			

May

M	T	W	T	F	S	S
				1	2	3
4	5	6	7	8	9	10
11	12	13	14	15	16	17
18	19	20	21	22	23	24
25	26	27	28	29	30	31

June

M	T	W	T	F	S	S
1	2	3	4	5	6	7
8	9	10	11	12	13	14
15	16	17	18	19	20	21
22	23	24	25	26	27	28
29	30					

July

M	T	W	T	F	S	S
		1	2	3	4	5
6	7	8	9	10	11	12
13	14	15	16	17	18	19
20	21	22	23	24	25	26
27	28	29	30	31		

August

M	T	W	T	F	S	S
					1	2
3	4	5	6	7	8	9
10	11	12	13	14	15	16
17	18	19	20	21	22	23
24	25	26	27	28	29	30
31						

September

M	T	W	T	F	S	S
	1	2	3	4	5	6
7	8	9	10	11	12	13
14	15	16	17	18	19	20
21	22	23	24	25	26	27
28	29	30				

October

M	T	W	T	F	S	S
			1	2	3	4
5	6	7	8	9	10	11
12	13	14	15	16	17	18
19	20	21	22	23	24	25
26	27	28	29	30	31	

November

M	T	W	T	F	S	S
						1
2	3	4	5	6	7	8
9	10	11	12	13	14	15
16	17	18	19	20	21	22
23	24	25	26	27	28	29
30						

December

M	T	W	T	F	S	S
	1	2	3	4	5	6
7	8	9	10	11	12	13
14	15	16	17	18	19	20
21	22	23	24	25	26	27
28	29	30	31			

2021 Calendar

January

M	T	W	T	F	S	S
				1	2	3
4	5	6	7	8	9	10
11	12	13	14	15	16	17
18	19	20	21	22	23	24
25	26	27	28	29	30	31

February

M	T	W	T	F	S	S
1	2	3	4	5	6	7
8	9	10	11	12	13	14
15	16	17	18	19	20	21
22	23	24	25	26	27	28

March

M	T	W	T	F	S	S
1	2	3	4	5	6	7
8	9	10	11	12	13	14
15	16	17	18	19	20	21
22	23	24	25	26	27	28
29	30	31				

April

M	T	W	T	F	S	S
			1	2	3	4
5	6	7	8	9	10	11
12	13	14	15	16	17	18
19	20	21	22	23	24	25
26	27	28	29	30		

May

M	T	W	T	F	S	S
					1	2
3	4	5	6	7	8	9
10	11	12	13	14	15	16
17	18	19	20	21	22	23
24	25	26	27	28	29	30
31						

June

M	T	W	T	F	S	S
	1	2	3	4	5	6
7	8	9	10	11	12	13
14	15	16	17	18	19	20
21	22	23	24	25	26	27
28	29	30				

July

M	T	W	T	F	S	S
			1	2	3	4
5	6	7	8	9	10	11
12	13	14	15	16	17	18
19	20	21	22	23	24	25
26	27	28	29	30	31	

August

M	T	W	T	F	S	S
						1
2	3	4	5	6	7	8
9	10	11	12	13	14	15
16	17	18	19	20	21	22
23	24	25	26	27	28	29
30	31					

September

M	T	W	T	F	S	S
		1	2	3	4	5
6	7	8	9	10	11	12
13	14	15	16	17	18	19
20	21	22	23	24	25	26
27	28	29	30			

October

M	T	W	T	F	S	S
				1	2	3
4	5	6	7	8	9	10
11	12	13	14	15	16	17
18	19	20	21	22	23	24
25	26	27	28	29	30	31

November

M	T	W	T	F	S	S
1	2	3	4	5	6	7
8	9	10	11	12	13	14
15	16	17	18	19	20	21
22	23	24	25	26	27	28
29	30					

December

M	T	W	T	F	S	S
		1	2	3	4	5
6	7	8	9	10	11	12
13	14	15	16	17	18	19
20	21	22	23	24	25	26
27	28	29	30	31		

2022 Calendar

January

M	T	W	T	F	S	S
					1	2
3	4	5	6	7	8	9
10	11	12	13	14	15	16
17	18	19	20	21	22	23
24	25	26	27	28	29	30
31						

February

M	T	W	T	F	S	S
	1	2	3	4	5	6
7	8	9	10	11	12	13
14	15	16	17	18	19	20
21	22	23	24	25	26	27
28						

March

M	T	W	T	F	S	S
	1	2	3	4	5	6
7	8	9	10	11	12	13
14	15	16	17	18	19	20
21	22	23	24	25	26	27
28	29	30	31			

April

M	T	W	T	F	S	S
				1	2	3
4	5	6	7	8	9	10
11	12	13	14	15	16	17
18	19	20	21	22	23	24
25	26	27	28	29	30	

May

M	T	W	T	F	S	S
						1
2	3	4	5	6	7	8
9	10	11	12	13	14	15
16	17	18	19	20	21	22
23	24	25	26	27	28	29
30	31					

June

M	T	W	T	F	S	S
		1	2	3	4	5
6	7	8	9	10	11	12
13	14	15	16	17	18	19
20	21	22	23	24	25	26
27	28	29	30			

July

M	T	W	T	F	S	S
				1	2	3
4	5	6	7	8	9	10
11	12	13	14	15	16	17
18	19	20	21	22	23	24
25	26	27	28	29	30	31

August

M	T	W	T	F	S	S
1	2	3	4	5	6	7
8	9	10	11	12	13	14
15	16	17	18	19	20	21
22	23	24	25	26	27	28
29	30	31				

September

M	T	W	T	F	S	S
			1	2	3	4
5	6	7	8	9	10	11
12	13	14	15	16	17	18
19	20	21	22	23	24	25
26	27	28	29	30		

October

M	T	W	T	F	S	S
					1	2
3	4	5	6	7	8	9
10	11	12	13	14	15	16
17	18	19	20	21	22	23
24	25	26	27	28	29	30
31						

November

M	T	W	T	F	S	S
	1	2	3	4	5	6
7	8	9	10	11	12	13
14	15	16	17	18	19	20
21	22	23	24	25	26	27
28	29	30				

December

M	T	W	T	F	S	S
			1	2	3	4
5	6	7	8	9	10	11
12	13	14	15	16	17	18
19	20	21	22	23	24	25
26	27	28	29	30	31	

Script Your Dream Life

Scripting is a Law of Attraction technique where you write a story about your life based on how you want it to be. Pretend you're writing your autobiography and you are writing the best version of your life story from this day forward. Write a story about your life based on how you want it to be.

Scripting is designed to help program both your conscious and subconscious mind by focusing on what it is you really want from life and how you will feel when these things arrive.

Close your eyes and see what you want to manifest. Visualize your dream life or goal. Imagine every aspect of your desire and see yourself with it. And then write it down in this journal. Journaling will raise your vibration.

The Law of Attraction responds to the thoughts you think, the words you speak and the emotions you feel.

DON'T FORGET – YOU ARE THE CREATOR OF YOUR OWN REALITY!

I am so happy and grateful now that

Vision Board

There's something magical about putting your big ideas, dreams and goals down on paper. Putting energy into a vision board will not only help you get crystal clear on what you want to create in your life but will also make your dreams come true.

SOMETIMES YOU HAVE TO SEE IT TO BELIEVE IT.

Having a visual reminder will help you stay focused and your vision board will also act as a benchmark for which you can measure your progress. It's always incredible to revisit an old vision board and realize all the dreams that have since come true!

Vision Board

My Journey

Write down your vision of where you want to go in each level of your life and write down how you will achieve your goals.

	WHERE AM I NOW?	WHERE DO I WANT TO BE?	HOW DO I GET THERE?
HEALTH			
SPIRITUAL			
CAREER			
RELATIONSHIP			
FAMILY			
FINANCES			
PERSONAL DEVELOPMENT			

My goats

Goal setting helps us create the markers and milestones along the way toward seeing our dreams come true.

Goals give us momentum to push through the adversity we experience while chasing our dreams.

SET GOALS IN ALL AREAS OF YOUR LIFE

1.	21.
2.	22.
3.	23.
4.	24.
5.	25.
6.	26.
7.	27.
8.	28.
9.	29.
10.	30.
11.	31.
12.	32.
13.	33.
14.	34.
15.	35.
16.	36.
17.	37.
18.	38.
19.	39.
20.	40.

2021
Goal setting

Decide your 5 most important one-year goals.

GOAL		WHY?
CHOOSE AND FOCUS ON TOP 5 GOALS FROM YOU LIST AND ASK YOURSELF – WHY ARE THESE GOALS IMPORTANT TO ME?		
1.		
2.		
3.		
4.		
5.		

Write down how you will reward yourself if you achieve your goals.

ACHIEVED		REWARD
SET REWARDS IF YOU ACHIEVE YOUR GOALS		
1.		
2.		
3.		
4.		
5.		

Mind map

Mind maps are powerful visual diagrams, they allow you to organize your thoughts. Best of all, a completed mind map offers you a higher-level perspective of your ideas in general. You'll likely gain important insight into your life just by writing out all of your goals in one place. Begin free-writing any thoughts, feelings, or observations about your: health, finances, family, spirituality, relationships, travel plans, your career and personal development goals.

To inspire ideas, ask yourself:
-What's most important to me about this part of my life and why?
-What would success ideally look like to me?
-What's the one thing I would change if I could?

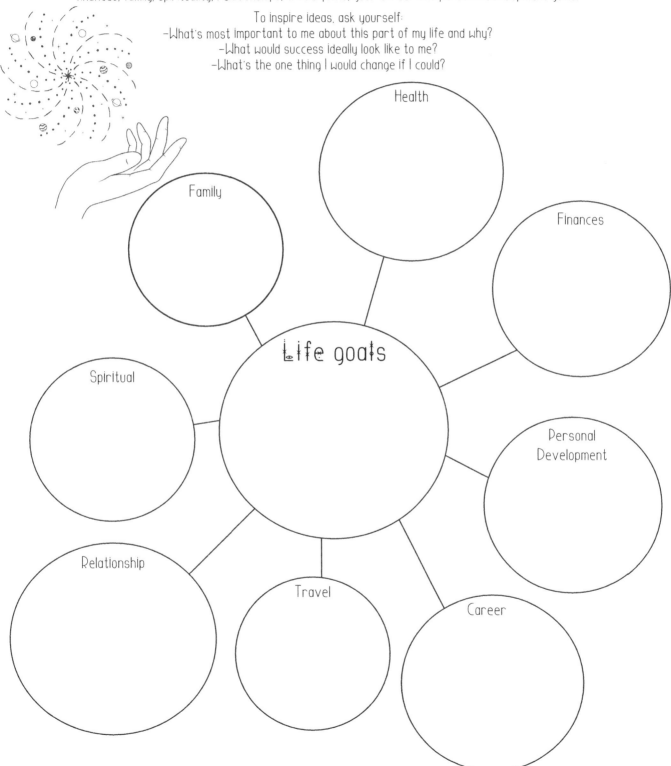

2021
Goal setting

Ask yourself — how will I make it happen?

Start taking action steps to achieve your goals.

MY GOAL	WHAT ARE MOST IMPORTANT STEPS TO MAKE IT HAPPEN?
	1. 2. 3. 4. 5.
	1. 2. 3. 4. 5.
	1. 2. 3. 4. 5.
	1. 2. 3. 4. 5.
	1. 2. 3. 4. 5.

Mind map your way to a successful year

Mind map and plan the upcoming year. Split each goal up into actionable tasks.
Track your progress and continue to check in throughout the year to see how you're doing.

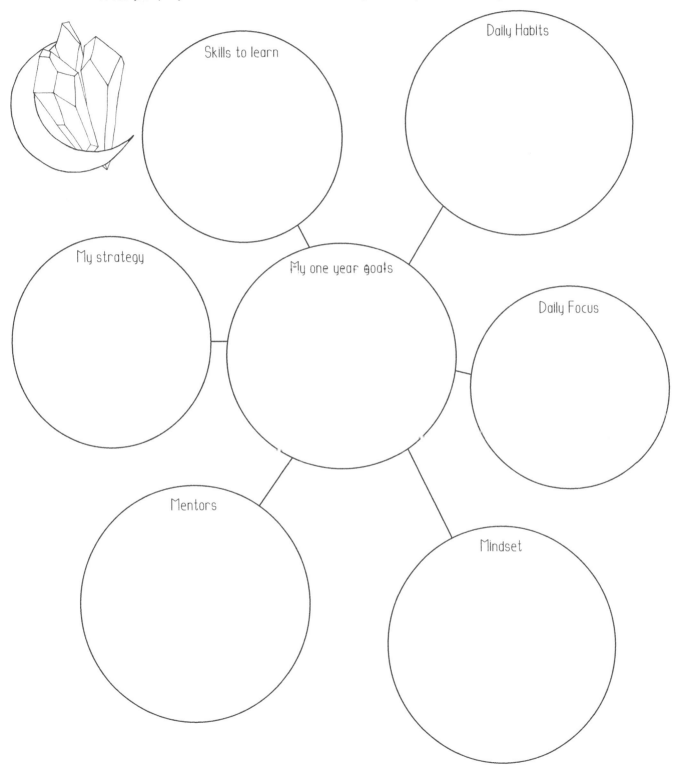

Skills to learn

Daily Habits

My strategy

My one year goals

Daily Focus

Mentors

Mindset

Reprogram your mind

MY FEARS	POSITIVE AFFIRMATIONS TO REPEAT DAILY
1.	
2.	
3.	
4.	
5.	

MY DISTRACTIONS	ACTION STEPS TO TAKE TO GET RID OF DISTRACTIONS
1.	
2.	
3.	
4.	
5.	

TOP 20 PLACES I WOULD LOVE TO VISIT

1.
2.
3.
4.
5.
6.
7.
8.
9.
10.
11.
12.
13.
14.
15.
16.
17.
18.
19.
20.

Write a Letter From Your Future Self

Writing down your goals from the perspective of the future — as if you've already succeeded in achieving them — is surprisingly therapeutic. If you visualise yourself in the place you want to be, it will help the Universe take you down that path.

"We receive exactly what we expect to receive."

— John Holland

I am so happy and grateful now that

2021

January

M	T	W	T	F	S	S
				1	2	3
4	5	6	7	8	9	10
11	12	13	14	15	16	17
18	19	20	21	22	23	24
25	26	27	28	29	30	31

Monthly Mood Tracker

Our Mood Tracker is a powerful and easy-to-use tool that allows you to track your emotions – or moods – on a regular basis.

You want to lead a fulfilling, happy life. All of that becomes so much simpler with the Mood Tracker. The perfect mental health support system, this Mood Tracker charts your triggers, looks at your ups and downs, and gives you permission to feel so you can understand your anxiety, support your stress relief, and become happier all around.

By tracking your moods, you may be able to determine situations or times that your mood goes up or down. Such situations are sometimes called triggers. For instance, if you notice you get depressed every time you visit your parents, that's important information that you can use to help you understand yourself better.

Reflect on emotions daily – gain insight into the patterns of your moods, triggers, coping skills, and mindsets.

Chart your emotions. Relieve your anxiety. BUILD A HAPPIER YOU!

COLOR YOUR MOOD

Angry	
Annoyed	
Anxious	
Ashamed	
Confused	
Energetic	
Excited	
Exhausted	
Happy	
Sad	
Relaxed	
Productive	

Monthly Goat Planner

GOAL

REWARD

∨	ACTION STEPS	NOTES

PROGRESS TRACKER

25%	50%	75%	100%

NOTES

GOAL

REWARD

∨	ACTION STEPS	NOTES

PROGRESS TRACKER

25%	50%	75%	100%

NOTES

Monthly Habit Tracker

Monthly habit tracker can be particularly powerful on a bad day. When you're feeling down, it's easy to forget about all the progress you have already made. Habit tracking provides visual proof of your hard work – a subtle reminder of how far you've come. Plus, the empty square you see each morning can motivate you to get started because you don't want to lose your progress by breaking your streak.

COLOR   ESSENTIAL HABITS

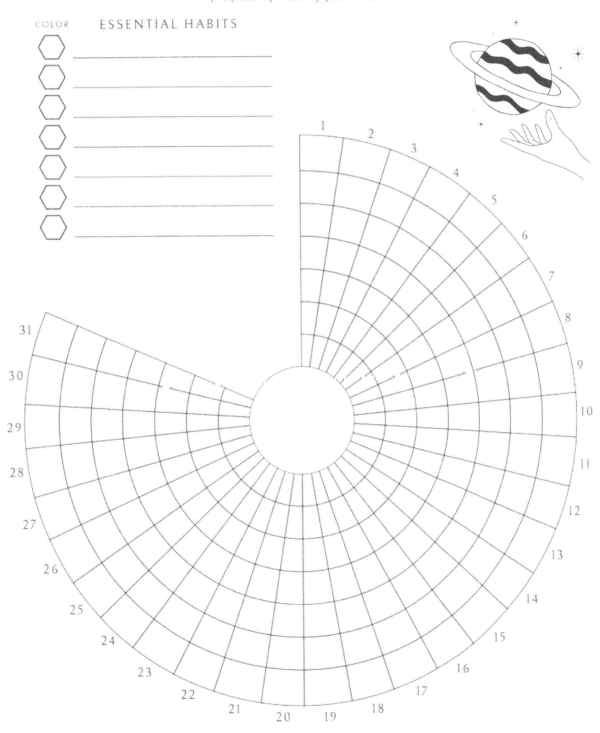

December 28–January 3

This week's priority

Top priority

....
....
....
....

Priority

....
....
....
....

Errands

....
....
....
....

Events | Appointments | Due dates

....
....
....
....
....
....
....
....
....
....

"Thoughts become things. If you see it in your mind,
you will hold it in your hand."

– Bob Proctor

notes | ideas

Positive Habits

	M	T	W	T	F	S	S
Gratitude							
Excercise							
Meditation							
Affirmations							

December

M	T	W	T	F	S	S
	1	2	3	4	5	6
7	8	9	10	11	12	13
14	15	16	17	18	19	20
21	22	23	24	25	26	27
28	29	30	31			

January

M	T	W	T	F	S	S
				1	2	3
4	5	6	7	8	9	10
11	12	13	14	15	16	17
18	19	20	21	22	23	24
25	26	27	28	29	30	31

Monday 28

TODAYS GOAL

PRIORITIES

1
2
3

5:00	
6:00	
7:00	
8:00	
9:00	
10:00	
11:00	
12:00	
1:00	
2:00	
3:00	
4:00	
5:00	
6:00	
7:00	
8:00	
9:00	
10:00	
11:00	

Tuesday 29

TODAYS GOAL

PRIORITIES

1
2
3

5:00	
6:00	
7:00	
8:00	
9:00	
10:00	
11:00	
12:00	
1:00	
2:00	
3:00	
4:00	
5:00	
6:00	
7:00	
8:00	
9:00	
10:00	
11:00	

Wednesday 30

TODAYS GOAL

PRIORITIES

1
2
3

5:00	
6:00	
7:00	
8:00	
9:00	
10:00	
11:00	
12:00	
1:00	
2:00	
3:00	
4:00	
5:00	
6:00	
7:00	
8:00	
9:00	
10:00	
11:00	

Thursday 31
New Year's Eve

TODAYS GOAL

PRIORITIES

1
2
3

5:00	
6:00	
7:00	
8:00	
9:00	
10:00	
11:00	
12:00	
1:00	
2:00	
3:00	
4:00	
5:00	
6:00	
7:00	
8:00	
9:00	
10:00	
11:00	

Friday 1
New Year's Day

TODAYS GOAL

PRIORITIES

1
2
3

5:00	
6:00	
7:00	
8:00	
9:00	
10:00	
11:00	
12:00	
1:00	
2:00	
3:00	
4:00	
5:00	
6:00	
7:00	
8:00	
9:00	
10:00	
11:00	

Saturday 2

TODAYS GOAL

PRIORITIES

1
2
3

5:00	
6:00	
7:00	
8:00	
9:00	
10:00	
11:00	
12:00	
1:00	
2:00	
3:00	
4:00	
5:00	
6:00	
7:00	
8:00	
9:00	
10:00	
11:00	

Sunday 3

TODAYS GOAL

PRIORITIES

1
2
3

5:00	
6:00	
7:00	
8:00	
9:00	
10:00	
11:00	
12:00	
1:00	
2:00	
3:00	
4:00	
5:00	
6:00	
7:00	
8:00	
9:00	
10:00	
11:00	

Gratitude box

January 4-10

This week's priority

....
....
....
....

Priority

....
....
....
....

Errands

....
....
....

Events | Appointments | Due dates

....
....
....
....
....
....
....
....
....
....
....
....

"What you think you become. What you feel you attract.
What you imagine you create."

– Buddha

notes | ideas

Positive Habits

	M	T	W	T	F	S	S
Gratitude							
Excercise							
Meditation							
Affirmations							

December

M	T	W	T	F	S	S
	1	2	3	4	5	6
7	8	9	10	11	12	13
14	15	16	17	18	19	20
21	22	23	24	25	26	27
28	29	30	31			

January

M	T	W	T	F	S	S
				1	2	3
4	5	6	7	8	9	10
11	12	13	14	15	16	17
18	19	20	21	22	23	24
25	26	27	28	29	30	31

Monday 4

TODAY'S GOAL

PRIORITIES

1
2
3

5:00
6:00
7:00
8:00
9:00
10:00
11:00
12:00
1:00
2:00
3:00
4:00
5:00
6:00
7:00
8:00
9:00
10:00
11:00

Tuesday 5

TODAY'S GOAL

PRIORITIES

1
2
3

5:00
6:00
7:00
8:00
9:00
10:00
11:00
12:00
1:00
2:00
3:00
4:00
5:00
6:00
7:00
8:00
9:00
10:00
11:00

Wednesday 6

TODAY'S GOAL

PRIORITIES

1
2
3

5:00
6:00
7:00
8:00
9:00
10:00
11:00
12:00
1:00
2:00
3:00
4:00
5:00
6:00
7:00
8:00
9:00
10:00
11:00

Thursday 7

TODAY'S GOAL

PRIORITIES

1
2
3

5:00
6:00
7:00
8:00
9:00
10:00
11:00
12:00
1:00
2:00
3:00
4:00
5:00
6:00
7:00
8:00
9:00
10:00
11:00

Friday 8

TODAY'S GOAL

PRIORITIES

1
2
3

5:00
6:00
7:00
8:00
9:00
10:00
11:00
12:00
1:00
2:00
3:00
4:00
5:00
6:00
7:00
8:00
9:00
10:00
11:00

Saturday 9

TODAY'S GOAL

PRIORITIES

1
2
3

5:00
6:00
7:00
8:00
9:00
10:00
11:00
12:00
1:00
2:00
3:00
4:00
5:00
6:00
7:00
8:00
9:00
10:00
11:00

Sunday 10

TODAY'S GOAL

PRIORITIES

1
2
3

5:00
6:00
7:00
8:00
9:00
10:00
11:00
12:00
1:00
2:00
3:00
4:00
5:00
6:00
7:00
8:00
9:00
10:00
11:00

Gratitude box

January 11-17

This week's priority

Top priority

....
....
....
....
....

Priority

....
....
....
....

Errands

....
....
....

Events † Appointments † Due dates

....
....
....
....
....
....
....
....
....
....
....
....

"Whether you think you can or think you can't, either way you are right."

— Henry Ford

notes † ideas

Positive Habits

	M	T	W	T	F	S	S
Gratitude							
Excercise							
Meditation							
Affirmations							

January

M	T	W	T	F	S	S
				1	2	3
4	5	6	7	8	9	10
11	12	13	14	15	16	17
18	19	20	21	22	23	24
25	26	27	28	29	30	31

February

M	T	W	T	F	S	S
1	2	3	4	5	6	7
8	9	10	11	12	13	14
15	16	17	18	19	20	21
22	23	24	25	26	27	28

Monday 11

TODAY'S GOAL

PRIORITIES
1
2
3

5:00	
6:00	
7:00	
8:00	
9:00	
10:00	
11:00	
12:00	
1:00	
2:00	
3:00	
4:00	
5:00	
6:00	
7:00	
8:00	
9:00	
10:00	
11:00	

Tuesday 12

TODAY'S GOAL

PRIORITIES
1
2
3

5:00	
6:00	
7:00	
8:00	
9:00	
10:00	
11:00	
12:00	
1:00	
2:00	
3:00	
4:00	
5:00	
6:00	
7:00	
8:00	
9:00	
10:00	
11:00	

Wednesday 13

TODAY'S GOAL

PRIORITIES
1
2
3

5:00	
6:00	
7:00	
8:00	
9:00	
10:00	
11:00	
12:00	
1:00	
2:00	
3:00	
4:00	
5:00	
6:00	
7:00	
8:00	
9:00	
10:00	
11:00	

Thursday 14

TODAY'S GOAL

PRIORITIES
1
2
3

5:00	
6:00	
7:00	
8:00	
9:00	
10:00	
11:00	
12:00	
1:00	
2:00	
3:00	
4:00	
5:00	
6:00	
7:00	
8:00	
9:00	
10:00	
11:00	

Friday 15

TODAY'S GOAL

PRIORITIES
1
2
3

5:00	
6:00	
7:00	
8:00	
9:00	
10:00	
11:00	
12:00	
1:00	
2:00	
3:00	
4:00	
5:00	
6:00	
7:00	
8:00	
9:00	
10:00	
11:00	

Saturday 16

TODAY'S GOAL

PRIORITIES
1
2
3

5:00	
6:00	
7:00	
8:00	
9:00	
10:00	
11:00	
12:00	
1:00	
2:00	
3:00	
4:00	
5:00	
6:00	
7:00	
8:00	
9:00	
10:00	
11:00	

Sunday 17

TODAY'S GOAL

PRIORITIES
1
2
3

5:00	
6:00	
7:00	
8:00	
9:00	
10:00	
11:00	
12:00	
1:00	
2:00	
3:00	
4:00	
5:00	
6:00	
7:00	
8:00	
9:00	
10:00	
11:00	

Gratitude box

January 18-24

This week's priority

Top priority

....
....
....
....

Priority

....
....
....
....

Errands

....
....
....

Events | Appointments | Due dates

....
....
....
....
....
....
....
....
....
....
....
....
....

"You create your thoughts, your thoughts create your intentions and your intentions create your reality."

– Wayne Dyer

notes | ideas

Positive Habits

	M	T	W	T	F	S	S
Gratitude							
Excercise							
Meditation							
Affirmations							

January

M	T	W	T	F	S	S
				1	2	3
4	5	6	7	8	9	10
11	12	13	14	15	16	17
18	19	20	21	22	23	24
25	26	27	28	29	30	31

February

M	T	W	T	F	S	S
1	2	3	4	5	6	7
8	9	10	11	12	13	14
15	16	17	18	19	20	21
22	23	24	25	26	27	28

Monday 18
Martin Luther King Jr Day

TODAY'S GOAL

PRIORITIES
1
2
3

5:00	
6:00	
7:00	
8:00	
9:00	
10:00	
11:00	
12:00	
1:00	
2:00	
3:00	
4:00	
5:00	
6:00	
7:00	
8:00	
9:00	
10:00	
11:00	

Tuesday 19

TODAY'S GOAL

PRIORITIES
1
2
3

5:00	
6:00	
7:00	
8:00	
9:00	
10:00	
11:00	
12:00	
1:00	
2:00	
3:00	
4:00	
5:00	
6:00	
7:00	
8:00	
9:00	
10:00	
11:00	

Wednesday 20

TODAY'S GOAL

PRIORITIES
1
2
3

5:00	
6:00	
7:00	
8:00	
9:00	
10:00	
11:00	
12:00	
1:00	
2:00	
3:00	
4:00	
5:00	
6:00	
7:00	
8:00	
9:00	
10:00	
11:00	

Thursday 21

TODAY'S GOAL

PRIORITIES
1
2
3

5:00	
6:00	
7:00	
8:00	
9:00	
10:00	
11:00	
12:00	
1:00	
2:00	
3:00	
4:00	
5:00	
6:00	
7:00	
8:00	
9:00	
10:00	
11:00	

Friday 22

TODAY'S GOAL

PRIORITIES
1
2
3

5:00	
6:00	
7:00	
8:00	
9:00	
10:00	
11:00	
12:00	
1:00	
2:00	
3:00	
4:00	
5:00	
6:00	
7:00	
8:00	
9:00	
10:00	
11:00	

Saturday 23

TODAY'S GOAL

PRIORITIES
1
2
3

5:00	
6:00	
7:00	
8:00	
9:00	
10:00	
11:00	
12:00	
1:00	
2:00	
3:00	
4:00	
5:00	
6:00	
7:00	
8:00	
9:00	
10:00	
11:00	

Sunday 24

TODAY'S GOAL

PRIORITIES
1
2
3

5:00	
6:00	
7:00	
8:00	
9:00	
10:00	
11:00	
12:00	
1:00	
2:00	
3:00	
4:00	
5:00	
6:00	
7:00	
8:00	
9:00	
10:00	
11:00	

Gratitude box

January 25-31

This week's priority

Top priority

....
....
....
....

Priority

....
....
....
....

Errands

....
....
....

Events | Appointments | Due dates

....
....
....
....
....
....
....
....
....
....

"Set your mind on a definite goal and observe how quickly the world
stands aside to let you pass."

– Napoleon Hill

notes | ideas

Positive Habits

	M	T	W	T	F	S	S
Gratitude							
Excercise							
Meditation							
Affirmations							

January

M	T	W	T	F	S	S
				1	2	3
4	5	6	7	8	9	10
11	12	13	14	15	16	17
18	19	20	21	22	23	24
25	26	27	28	29	30	31

February

M	T	W	T	F	S	S
1	2	3	4	5	6	7
8	9	10	11	12	13	14
15	16	17	18	19	20	21
22	23	24	25	26	27	28

Monday 25

TODAY'S GOAL

PRIORITIES
1
2
3

5.00	
6.00	
7.00	
8.00	
9.00	
10.00	
11.00	
12.00	
1.00	
2.00	
3.00	
4.00	
5.00	
6.00	
7.00	
8.00	
9.00	
10.00	
11.00	

Tuesday 26

TODAY'S GOAL

PRIORITIES
1
2
3

5.00	
6.00	
7.00	
8.00	
9.00	
10.00	
11.00	
12.00	
1.00	
2.00	
3.00	
4.00	
5.00	
6.00	
7.00	
8.00	
9.00	
10.00	
11.00	

Wednesday 27

TODAY'S GOAL

PRIORITIES
1
2
3

5.00	
6.00	
7.00	
8.00	
9.00	
10.00	
11.00	
12.00	
1.00	
2.00	
3.00	
4.00	
5.00	
6.00	
7.00	
8.00	
9.00	
10.00	
11.00	

Thursday 28

TODAY'S GOAL

PRIORITIES
1
2
3

5.00	
6.00	
7.00	
8.00	
9.00	
10.00	
11.00	
12.00	
1.00	
2.00	
3.00	
4.00	
5.00	
6.00	
7.00	
8.00	
9.00	
10.00	
11.00	

Friday 29

TODAY'S GOAL

PRIORITIES
1
2
3

5.00	
6.00	
7.00	
8.00	
9.00	
10.00	
11.00	
12.00	
1.00	
2.00	
3.00	
4.00	
5.00	
6.00	
7.00	
8.00	
9.00	
10.00	
11.00	

Saturday 30

TODAY'S GOAL

PRIORITIES
1
2
3

5.00	
6.00	
7.00	
8.00	
9.00	
10.00	
11.00	
12.00	
1.00	
2.00	
3.00	
4.00	
5.00	
6.00	
7.00	
8.00	
9.00	
10.00	
11.00	

Sunday 31

TODAY'S GOAL

PRIORITIES
1
2
3

5.00	
6.00	
7.00	
8.00	
9.00	
10.00	
11.00	
12.00	
1.00	
2.00	
3.00	
4.00	
5.00	
6.00	
7.00	
8.00	
9.00	
10.00	
11.00	

Gratitude box

Reflect on your month

When you start actively observing and understanding the invisible parts of yourself – your emotions – you'll equip yourself with the tools to make visible changes in your day-to-day life. Observe how your emotions and feelings change over weeks and months. Become aware of them and change them to more positive feelings so you can attract and manifest the life of your dreams.

Check how balanced you lived your month.

What did I learn this month?

....
....
....
....

My top 5 achievements this month

....
....
....
....

Did I enjoy what I was doing this month?

....
....
....
....
....

How did I make myself feel good?

....
....
....
....
....

How was I feeling this month?

Emotion wheel with inner segments: Happy, Sad, Disgust, Anger, Fear, Surprise. Outer emotions: Optimistic, Proud, Guilty, Depressed, Lonely, Disapproval, Awful, Disappointed, Aggressive, Mad, Hurt, Scared, Humiliated, Insecure, Amazed, Excited, Confused, Peaceful.

How do I feel about my progress this month?

_____
_____
_____
_____

What are the greatest insights that I have gained?

_____
_____
_____
_____

What mental blocks did I encounter?

_____
_____
_____
_____

What / who inspired me this month?

_____
_____
_____
_____

What actions can I take to improve?

_____
_____
_____
_____

2021

February

M	T	W	T	F	S	S
1	2	3	4	5	6	7
8	9	10	11	12	13	14
15	16	17	18	19	20	21
22	23	24	25	26	27	28

Monthly Mood Tracker

Our Mood Tracker is a powerful and easy-to-use tool that allows you to track your emotions – or moods – on a regular basis.

You want to lead a fulfilling, happy life. All of that becomes so much simpler with the Mood Tracker. The perfect mental health support system, this Mood Tracker charts your triggers, looks at your ups and downs, and gives you permission to feel so you can understand your anxiety, support your stress relief, and become happier all around.

By tracking your moods, you may be able to determine situations or times that your mood goes up or down. Such situations are sometimes called triggers. For instance, if you notice you get depressed every time you visit your parents, that's important information that you can use to help you understand yourself better.

Reflect on emotions daily – gain insight into the patterns of your moods, triggers, coping skills, and mindsets.

Chart your emotions. Relieve your anxiety. BUILD A HAPPIER YOU!

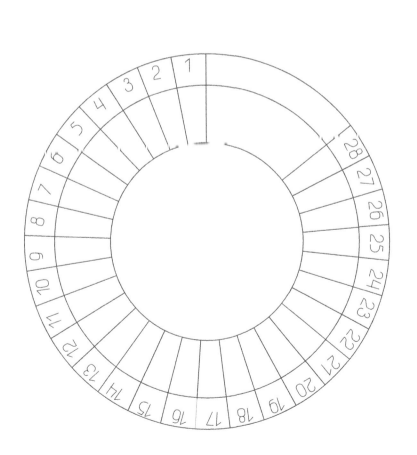

COLOR YOUR MOOD

Angry	
Annoyed	
Anxious	
Ashamed	
Confused	
Energetic	
Excited	
Exhausted	
Happy	
Sad	
Relaxed	
Productive	

Monthly Goal Planner

GOAL

REWARD

✓	ACTION STEPS	NOTES

PROGRESS TRACKER

| 25% | 50% | 75% | 100% |

NOTES

GOAL

REWARD

✓	ACTION STEPS	NOTES

PROGRESS TRACKER

| 25% | 50% | 75% | 100% |

NOTES

Monthly Habit Tracker

Monthly habit tracker can be particularly powerful on a bad day. When you're feeling down, it's easy to forget about all the progress you have already made. Habit tracking provides visual proof of your hard work — a subtle reminder of how far you've come. Plus, the empty square you see each morning can motivate you to get started because you don't want to lose your progress by breaking your streak.

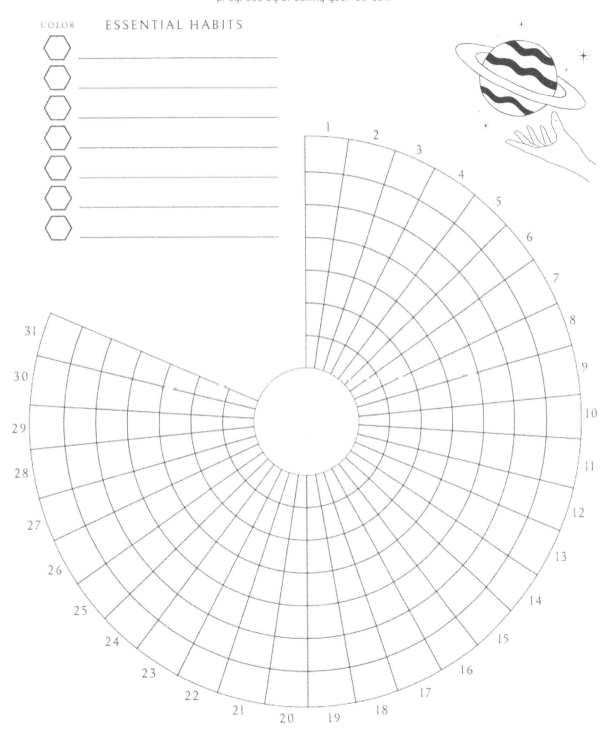

COLOR   ESSENTIAL HABITS

February 1-7

This week's priority

Top priority
....
....
....
....

Priority
....
....
....
....

Errands
....
....
....

Events | Appointments | Due dates
....
....
....
....
....
....
....
....

"We often become what we believe ourselves to be. If I believe I cannot do something, it makes me incapable of doing it. When I believe I can, I acquire the ability to do it, even if I didn't have it in the beginning."

— Gandhi

notes | ideas

Positive Habits

	M	T	W	T	F	S	S
Gratitude							
Excercise							
Meditation							
Affirmations							

January

M	T	W	T	F	S	S
				1	2	3
4	5	6	7	8	9	10
11	12	13	14	15	16	17
18	19	20	21	22	23	24
25	26	27	28	29	30	31

February

M	T	W	T	F	S	S
1	2	3	4	5	6	7
8	9	10	11	12	13	14
15	16	17	18	19	20	21
22	23	24	25	26	27	28

Monday · 1

TODAY'S GOAL

PRIORITIES
1
2
3

5:00	
6:00	
7:00	
8:00	
9:00	
10:00	
11:00	
12:00	
1:00	
2:00	
3:00	
4:00	
5:00	
6:00	
7:00	
8:00	
9:00	
10:00	
11:00	

Tuesday · 2

TODAY'S GOAL

PRIORITIES
1
2
3

5:00	
6:00	
7:00	
8:00	
9:00	
10:00	
11:00	
12:00	
1:00	
2:00	
3:00	
4:00	
5:00	
6:00	
7:00	
8:00	
9:00	
10:00	
11:00	

Wednesday · 3

TODAY'S GOAL

PRIORITIES
1
2
3

5:00	
6:00	
7:00	
8:00	
9:00	
10:00	
11:00	
12:00	
1:00	
2:00	
3:00	
4:00	
5:00	
6:00	
7:00	
8:00	
9:00	
10:00	
11:00	

Thursday · 4

TODAY'S GOAL

PRIORITIES
1
2
3

5:00	
6:00	
7:00	
8:00	
9:00	
10:00	
11:00	
12:00	
1:00	
2:00	
3:00	
4:00	
5:00	
6:00	
7:00	
8:00	
9:00	
10:00	
11:00	

Friday · 5

TODAY'S GOAL

PRIORITIES
1
2
3

5:00	
6:00	
7:00	
8:00	
9:00	
10:00	
11:00	
12:00	
1:00	
2:00	
3:00	
4:00	
5:00	
6:00	
7:00	
8:00	
9:00	
10:00	
11:00	

Saturday · 6

TODAY'S GOAL

PRIORITIES
1
2
3

5:00	
6:00	
7:00	
8:00	
9:00	
10:00	
11:00	
12:00	
1:00	
2:00	
3:00	
4:00	
5:00	
6:00	
7:00	
8:00	
9:00	
10:00	
11:00	

Sunday · 7

TODAY'S GOAL

PRIORITIES
1
2
3

5:00	
6:00	
7:00	
8:00	
9:00	
10:00	
11:00	
12:00	
1:00	
2:00	
3:00	
4:00	
5:00	
6:00	
7:00	
8:00	
9:00	
10:00	
11:00	

Gratitude box

February 8-14

This week's priority

Top priority

....
....
....
....

Priority

....
....
....
....

Errands

....
....
....

Events | Appointments | Due dates

....
....
....
....
....
....
....
....

"The law of attraction states that whatever you focus on, think about, read about, and talk about intensely, you're going to attract more of into your life."

– Jack Canfield

notes | ideas

Positive Habits

	M	T	W	T	F	S	S
Gratitude							
Excercise							
Meditation							
Affirmations							

January

M	T	W	T	F	S	S
				1	2	3
4	5	6	7	8	9	10
11	12	13	14	15	16	17
18	19	20	21	22	23	24
25	26	27	28	29	30	31

February

M	T	W	T	F	S	S
1	2	3	4	5	6	7
8	9	10	11	12	13	14
15	16	17	18	19	20	21
22	23	24	25	26	27	28

Monday 8

TODAY'S GOAL

PRIORITIES
1
2
3

| 5:00 |
| 6:00 |
| 7:00 |
| 8:00 |
| 9:00 |
| 10:00 |
| 11:00 |
| 12:00 |
| 1:00 |
| 2:00 |
| 3:00 |
| 4:00 |
| 5:00 |
| 6:00 |
| 7:00 |
| 8:00 |
| 9:00 |
| 10:00 |
| 11:00 |

Tuesday 9

TODAY'S GOAL

PRIORITIES
1
2
3

| 5:00 |
| 6:00 |
| 7:00 |
| 8:00 |
| 9:00 |
| 10:00 |
| 11:00 |
| 12:00 |
| 1:00 |
| 2:00 |
| 3:00 |
| 4:00 |
| 5:00 |
| 6:00 |
| 7:00 |
| 8:00 |
| 9:00 |
| 10:00 |
| 11:00 |

Wednesday 10

TODAY'S GOAL

PRIORITIES
1
2
3

| 5:00 |
| 6:00 |
| 7:00 |
| 8:00 |
| 9:00 |
| 10:00 |
| 11:00 |
| 12:00 |
| 1:00 |
| 2:00 |
| 3:00 |
| 4:00 |
| 5:00 |
| 6:00 |
| 7:00 |
| 8:00 |
| 9:00 |
| 10:00 |
| 11:00 |

Thursday 11

TODAY'S GOAL

PRIORITIES
1
2
3

| 5:00 |
| 6:00 |
| 7:00 |
| 8:00 |
| 9:00 |
| 10:00 |
| 11:00 |
| 12:00 |
| 1:00 |
| 2:00 |
| 3:00 |
| 4:00 |
| 5:00 |
| 6:00 |
| 7:00 |
| 8:00 |
| 9:00 |
| 10:00 |
| 11:00 |

Friday 12

TODAY'S GOAL

PRIORITIES
1
2
3

| 5:00 |
| 6:00 |
| 7:00 |
| 8:00 |
| 9:00 |
| 10:00 |
| 11:00 |
| 12:00 |
| 1:00 |
| 2:00 |
| 3:00 |
| 4:00 |
| 5:00 |
| 6:00 |
| 7:00 |
| 8:00 |
| 9:00 |
| 10:00 |
| 11:00 |

Saturday 13

TODAY'S GOAL

PRIORITIES
1
2
3

| 5:00 |
| 6:00 |
| 7:00 |
| 8:00 |
| 9:00 |
| 10:00 |
| 11:00 |
| 12:00 |
| 1:00 |
| 2:00 |
| 3:00 |
| 4:00 |
| 5:00 |
| 6:00 |
| 7:00 |
| 8:00 |
| 9:00 |
| 10:00 |
| 11:00 |

Sunday 14

Valentine's Day

TODAY'S GOAL

PRIORITIES
1
2
3

| 5:00 |
| 6:00 |
| 7:00 |
| 8:00 |
| 9:00 |
| 10:00 |
| 11:00 |
| 12:00 |
| 1:00 |
| 2:00 |
| 3:00 |
| 4:00 |
| 5:00 |
| 6:00 |
| 7:00 |
| 8:00 |
| 9:00 |
| 10:00 |
| 11:00 |

Gratitude box

February 15-21

This week's priority

Top priority

....
....
....
....

Priority

....
....
....
....

Errands

....
....
....

Events | Appointments | Due dates

....
....
....
....
....
....
....
....
....

"Whatever you hold in your mind on a consistent basis is exactly what you will experience in your life."

— Tony Robbins

notes | ideas

Positive Habits

	M	T	W	T	F	S	S
Gratitude							
Excercise							
Meditation							
Affirmations							

February

M	T	W	T	F	S	S
1	2	3	4	5	6	7
8	9	10	11	12	13	14
15	16	17	18	19	20	21
22	23	24	25	26	27	28

March

M	T	W	T	F	S	S
1	2	3	4	5	6	7
8	9	10	11	12	13	14
15	16	17	18	19	20	21
22	23	24	25	26	27	28
29	30	31				

Monday 15

TODAY'S GOAL

PRIORITIES
1
2
3

5:00	
6:00	
7:00	
8:00	
9:00	
10:00	
11:00	
12:00	
1:00	
2:00	
3:00	
4:00	
5:00	
6:00	
7:00	
8:00	
9:00	
10:00	
11:00	

Tuesday 16

TODAY'S GOAL

PRIORITIES
1
2
3

5:00	
6:00	
7:00	
8:00	
9:00	
10:00	
11:00	
12:00	
1:00	
2:00	
3:00	
4:00	
5:00	
6:00	
7:00	
8:00	
9:00	
10:00	
11:00	

Wednesday 17

TODAY'S GOAL

PRIORITIES
1
2
3

5:00	
6:00	
7:00	
8:00	
9:00	
10:00	
11:00	
12:00	
1:00	
2:00	
3:00	
4:00	
5:00	
6:00	
7:00	
8:00	
9:00	
10:00	
11:00	

Thursday 18

TODAY'S GOAL

PRIORITIES
1
2
3

5:00	
6:00	
7:00	
8:00	
9:00	
10:00	
11:00	
12:00	
1:00	
2:00	
3:00	
4:00	
5:00	
6:00	
7:00	
8:00	
9:00	
10:00	
11:00	

Friday 19

TODAY'S GOAL

PRIORITIES
1
2
3

5:00	
6:00	
7:00	
8:00	
9:00	
10:00	
11:00	
12:00	
1:00	
2:00	
3:00	
4:00	
5:00	
6:00	
7:00	
8:00	
9:00	
10:00	
11:00	

Saturday 20

TODAY'S GOAL

PRIORITIES
1
2
3

5:00	
6:00	
7:00	
8:00	
9:00	
10:00	
11:00	
12:00	
1:00	
2:00	
3:00	
4:00	
5:00	
6:00	
7:00	
8:00	
9:00	
10:00	
11:00	

Sunday 21

TODAY'S GOAL

PRIORITIES
1
2
3

5:00	
6:00	
7:00	
8:00	
9:00	
10:00	
11:00	
12:00	
1:00	
2:00	
3:00	
4:00	
5:00	
6:00	
7:00	
8:00	
9:00	
10:00	
11:00	

Gratitude box

February 22-28

This week's priority

Top priority
....
....
....
....

Priority
....
....
....
....

Errands
....
....
....

Events | Appointments | Due dates

....
....
....
....
....
....
....
....
....
....

"Your whole life is a manifestation of the thoughts that go on in your head."

– Lisa Nichols

notes | ideas

Positive Habits

	M	T	W	T	F	S	S
Gratitude							
Excercise							
Meditation							
Affirmations							

February

M	T	W	T	F	S	S
1	2	3	4	5	6	7
8	9	10	11	12	13	14
15	16	17	18	19	20	21
22	23	24	25	26	27	28

March

M	T	W	T	F	S	S
1	2	3	4	5	6	7
8	9	10	11	12	13	14
15	16	17	18	19	20	21
22	23	24	25	26	27	28
29	30	31				

Monday 22

TODAY'S GOAL

PRIORITIES
1
2
3

5:00	
6:00	
7:00	
8:00	
9:00	
10:00	
11:00	
12:00	
1:00	
2:00	
3:00	
4:00	
5:00	
6:00	
7:00	
8:00	
9:00	
10:00	
11:00	

Tuesday 23

TODAY'S GOAL

PRIORITIES
1
2
3

5:00	
6:00	
7:00	
8:00	
9:00	
10:00	
11:00	
12:00	
1:00	
2:00	
3:00	
4:00	
5:00	
6:00	
7:00	
8:00	
9:00	
10:00	
11:00	

Wednesday 24

TODAY'S GOAL

PRIORITIES
1
2
3

5:00	
6:00	
7:00	
8:00	
9:00	
10:00	
11:00	
12:00	
1:00	
2:00	
3:00	
4:00	
5:00	
6:00	
7:00	
8:00	
9:00	
10:00	
11:00	

Thursday 25

TODAY'S GOAL

PRIORITIES
1
2
3

5:00	
6:00	
7:00	
8:00	
9:00	
10:00	
11:00	
12:00	
1:00	
2:00	
3:00	
4:00	
5:00	
6:00	
7:00	
8:00	
9:00	
10:00	
11:00	

Friday 26

TODAY'S GOAL

PRIORITIES
1
2
3

5:00	
6:00	
7:00	
8:00	
9:00	
10:00	
11:00	
12:00	
1:00	
2:00	
3:00	
4:00	
5:00	
6:00	
7:00	
8:00	
9:00	
10:00	
11:00	

Saturday 27

TODAY'S GOAL

PRIORITIES
1
2
3

5:00	
6:00	
7:00	
8:00	
9:00	
10:00	
11:00	
12:00	
1:00	
2:00	
3:00	
4:00	
5:00	
6:00	
7:00	
8:00	
9:00	
10:00	
11:00	

Sunday 28

TODAY'S GOAL

PRIORITIES
1
2
3

5:00	
6:00	
7:00	
8:00	
9:00	
10:00	
11:00	
12:00	
1:00	
2:00	
3:00	
4:00	
5:00	
6:00	
7:00	
8:00	
9:00	
10:00	
11:00	

Gratitude box

Reflect on your month

When you start actively observing and understanding the invisible parts of yourself – your emotions – you'll equip yourself with the tools to make visible changes in your day-to-day life. Observe how your emotions and feelings change over weeks and months. Become aware of them and change them to more positive feelings so you can attract and manifest the life of your dreams.

Check how balanced you lived your month.

What did I learn this month?

....
....
....
....
....

My top 5 achievements this month

....
....
....
....

How was I feeling this month?

Optimistic, Proud, Guilty, Depressed, Peaceful, Lonely, Confused, Happy, Sad, Disapproval, Excited, Surprise, Disgust, Awful, Amazed, Fear, Anger, Disappointed, Insecure, Humiliated, Scared, Hurt, Mad, Aggressive

Did I enjoy what I was doing this month?

....
....
....
....
....

How did I make myself feel good?

....
....
....
....
....

How do I feel about my progress this month?

....
....
....
....
....

What are the greatest insights that I have gained?

....
....
....
....
....

What mental blocks did I encounter?

....
....
....
....
....

What / who inspired me this month?

....
....
....
....
....

What actions can I take to improve?

....
....
....
....

2021

March

M	T	W	T	F	S	S
1	2	3	4	5	6	7
8	9	10	11	12	13	14
15	16	17	18	19	20	21
22	23	24	25	26	27	28
29	30	31				

Monthly Mood Tracker

Our Mood Tracker is a powerful and easy-to-use tool that allows you to track your emotions – or moods – on a regular basis.

You want to lead a fulfilling, happy life. All of that becomes so much simpler with the Mood Tracker. The perfect mental health support system, this Mood Tracker charts your triggers, looks at your ups and downs, and gives you permission to feel so you can understand your anxiety, support your stress relief, and become happier all around.

By tracking your moods, you may be able to determine situations or times that your mood goes up or down. Such situations are sometimes called triggers. For instance, if you notice you get depressed every time you visit your parents, that's important information that you can use to help you understand yourself better.

Reflect on emotions daily – gain insight into the patterns of your moods, triggers, coping skills, and mindsets.

Chart your emotions. Relieve your anxiety. BUILD A HAPPIER YOU!

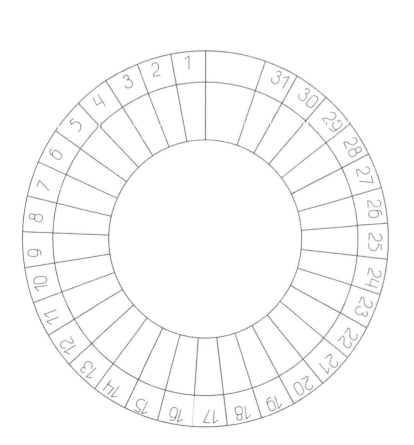

COLOR YOUR MOOD

Angry	
Annoyed	
Anxious	
Ashamed	
Confused	
Energetic	
Excited	
Exhausted	
Happy	
Sad	
Relaxed	
Productive	

Monthly Goal Planner

GOAL

REWARD

✔	ACTION STEPS	NOTES

PROGRESS TRACKER

25%　　　　　　50%　　　　　　75%　　　　　　100%

NOTES

GOAL

REWARD

✔	ACTION STEPS	NOTES

PROGRESS TRACKER

25%　　　　　　50%　　　　　　75%　　　　　　100%

NOTES

Monthly Habit Tracker

Monthly habit tracker can be particularly powerful on a bad day. When you're feeling down, it's easy to forget about all the progress you have already made. Habit tracking provides visual proof of your hard work — a subtle reminder of how far you've come. Plus, the empty square you see each morning can motivate you to get started because you don't want to lose your progress by breaking your streak.

COLOR   ESSENTIAL HABITS

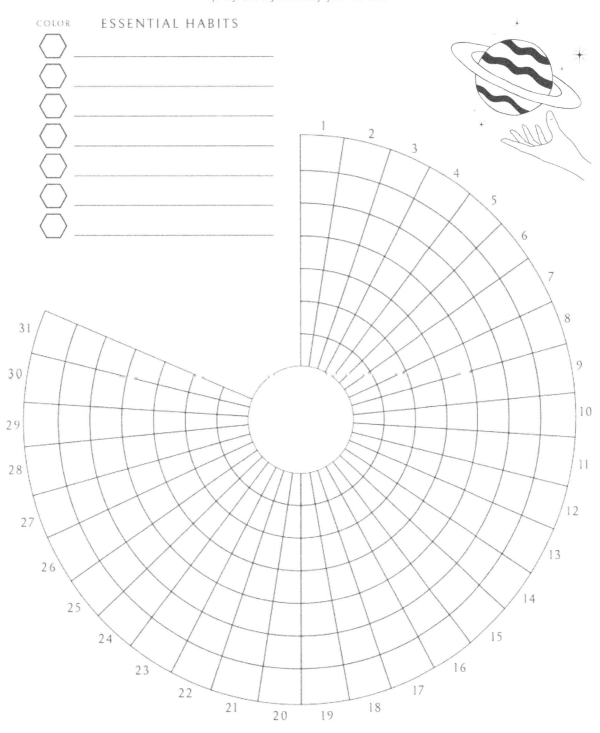

March 1-7

This week's priority

Top priority
....
....
....

Priority
....
....
....

Errands
....
....

Events | Appointments | Due dates

....
....
....
....
....
....
....
....
....
....
....

"Beware of what you set your heart upon...for it shall surely be yours."

– Ralph Waldo Emerson

notes | ideas

Positive Habits

	M	T	W	T	F	S	S
Gratitude							
Excercise							
Meditation							
Affirmations							

February

M	T	W	T	F	S	S
1	2	3	4	5	6	7
8	9	10	11	12	13	14
15	16	17	18	19	20	21
22	23	24	25	26	27	28

March

M	T	W	T	F	S	S
1	2	3	4	5	6	7
8	9	10	11	12	13	14
15	16	17	18	19	20	21
22	23	24	25	26	27	28
29	30	31				

Monday 1

TODAY'S GOAL

PRIORITIES
1
2
3

5.00	
6.00	
7.00	
8.00	
9.00	
10.00	
11.00	
12.00	
1.00	
2.00	
3.00	
4.00	
5.00	
6.00	
7.00	
8.00	
9.00	
10.00	
11.00	

Tuesday 2

TODAY'S GOAL

PRIORITIES
1
2
3

5.00	
6.00	
7.00	
8.00	
9.00	
10.00	
11.00	
12.00	
1.00	
2.00	
3.00	
4.00	
5.00	
6.00	
7.00	
8.00	
9.00	
10.00	
11.00	

Wednesday 3

TODAY'S GOAL

PRIORITIES
1
2
3

5.00	
6.00	
7.00	
8.00	
9.00	
10.00	
11.00	
12.00	
1.00	
2.00	
3.00	
4.00	
5.00	
6.00	
7.00	
8.00	
9.00	
10.00	
11.00	

Thursday 4

TODAY'S GOAL

PRIORITIES
1
2
3

5.00	
6.00	
7.00	
8.00	
9.00	
10.00	
11.00	
12.00	
1.00	
2.00	
3.00	
4.00	
5.00	
6.00	
7.00	
8.00	
9.00	
10.00	
11.00	

Friday 5

TODAY'S GOAL

PRIORITIES
1
2
3

5.00	
6.00	
7.00	
8.00	
9.00	
10.00	
11.00	
12.00	
1.00	
2.00	
3.00	
4.00	
5.00	
6.00	
7.00	
8.00	
9.00	
10.00	
11.00	

Saturday 6

TODAY'S GOAL

PRIORITIES
1
2
3

5.00	
6.00	
7.00	
8.00	
9.00	
10.00	
11.00	
12.00	
1.00	
2.00	
3.00	
4.00	
5.00	
6.00	
7.00	
8.00	
9.00	
10.00	
11.00	

Sunday 7

TODAY'S GOAL

PRIORITIES
1
2
3

5.00	
6.00	
7.00	
8.00	
9.00	
10.00	
11.00	
12.00	
1.00	
2.00	
3.00	
4.00	
5.00	
6.00	
7.00	
8.00	
9.00	
10.00	
11.00	

Gratitude box

March 8-14

This week's priority

Top priority

....
....
....
....
....

Priority

....
....
....
....

Errands

....
....
....

Events | Appointments | Due dates

....
....
....
....
....
....
....
....

"Everything is energy and that's all there is to it. Match the frequency of
the reality you want and you cannot help but get that reality. It can be no
other way. This is not philosophy. This is physics."

— Albert Einstein

notes | ideas

Positive Habits

	M	T	W	T	F	S	S
Gratitude							
Excercise							
Meditation							
Affirmations							

February

M	T	W	T	F	S	S
1	2	3	4	5	6	7
8	9	10	11	12	13	14
15	16	17	18	19	20	21
22	23	24	25	26	27	28

March

M	T	W	T	F	S	S
1	2	3	4	5	6	7
8	9	10	11	12	13	14
15	16	17	18	19	20	21
22	23	24	25	26	27	28
29	30	31				

Monday 8

TODAY'S GOAL

PRIORITIES

1
2
3

5.00
6.00
7.00
8.00
9.00
10.00
11.00
12.00
1.00
2.00
3.00
4.00
5.00
6.00
7.00
8.00
9.00
10.00
11.00

Tuesday 9

TODAY'S GOAL

PRIORITIES

1
2
3

5.00
6.00
7.00
8.00
9.00
10.00
11.00
12.00
1.00
2.00
3.00
4.00
5.00
6.00
7.00
8.00
9.00
10.00
11.00

Wednesday 10

TODAY'S GOAL

PRIORITIES

1
2
3

5.00
6.00
7.00
8.00
9.00
10.00
11.00
12.00
1.00
2.00
3.00
4.00
5.00
6.00
7.00
8.00
9.00
10.00
11.00

Thursday 11

TODAY'S GOAL

PRIORITIES

1
2
3

5.00
6.00
7.00
8.00
9.00
10.00
11.00
12.00
1.00
2.00
3.00
4.00
5.00
6.00
7.00
8.00
9.00
10.00
11.00

Friday 12

TODAY'S GOAL

PRIORITIES

1
2
3

5.00
6.00
7.00
8.00
9.00
10.00
11.00
12.00
1.00
2.00
3.00
4.00
5.00
6.00
7.00
8.00
9.00
10.00
11.00

Saturday 13

TODAY'S GOAL

PRIORITIES

1
2
3

5.00
6.00
7.00
8.00
9.00
10.00
11.00
12.00
1.00
2.00
3.00
4.00
5.00
6.00
7.00
8.00
9.00
10.00
11.00

Sunday 14

TODAY'S GOAL

PRIORITIES

1
2
3

5.00
6.00
7.00
8.00
9.00
10.00
11.00
12.00
1.00
2.00
3.00
4.00
5.00
6.00
7.00
8.00
9.00
10.00
11.00

Gratitude box

March 15–21

This week's priority

Top priority

....
....
....
....

Priority

....
....
....
....

Errands

....
....
....

Events | Appointments | Due dates

....
....
....
....
....
....
....
....
....
....

"Ask for what you want and be prepared to get it."

– Maya Angelou

notes | ideas

Positive Habits

	M	T	W	T	F	S	S
Gratitude							
Excercise							
Meditation							
Affirmations							

February

M	T	W	T	F	S	S
1	2	3	4	5	6	7
8	9	10	11	12	13	14
15	16	17	18	19	20	21
22	23	24	25	26	27	28

March

M	T	W	T	F	S	S
1	2	3	4	5	6	7
8	9	10	11	12	13	14
15	16	17	18	19	20	21
22	23	24	25	26	27	28
29	30	31				

Monday 15

TODAY'S GOAL

PRIORITIES

1
2
3

Time	
5:00	
6:00	
7:00	
8:00	
9:00	
10:00	
11:00	
12:00	
1:00	
2:00	
3:00	
4:00	
5:00	
6:00	
7:00	
8:00	
9:00	
10:00	
11:00	

Tuesday 16

TODAY'S GOAL

PRIORITIES

1
2
3

Time	
5:00	
6:00	
7:00	
8:00	
9:00	
10:00	
11:00	
12:00	
1:00	
2:00	
3:00	
4:00	
5:00	
6:00	
7:00	
8:00	
9:00	
10:00	
11:00	

Wednesday 17

St. Patrick's Day

TODAY'S GOAL

PRIORITIES

1
2
3

Time	
5:00	
6:00	
7:00	
8:00	
9:00	
10:00	
11:00	
12:00	
1:00	
2:00	
3:00	
4:00	
5:00	
6:00	
7:00	
8:00	
9:00	
10:00	
11:00	

Thursday 18

TODAY'S GOAL

PRIORITIES

1
2
3

Time	
5:00	
6:00	
7:00	
8:00	
9:00	
10:00	
11:00	
12:00	
1:00	
2:00	
3:00	
4:00	
5:00	
6:00	
7:00	
8:00	
9:00	
10:00	
11:00	

Friday 19

TODAY'S GOAL

PRIORITIES

1
2
3

Time	
5:00	
6:00	
7:00	
8:00	
9:00	
10:00	
11:00	
12:00	
1:00	
2:00	
3:00	
4:00	
5:00	
6:00	
7:00	
8:00	
9:00	
10:00	
11:00	

Saturday 20

TODAY'S GOAL

PRIORITIES

1
2
3

Time	
5:00	
6:00	
7:00	
8:00	
9:00	
10:00	
11:00	
12:00	
1:00	
2:00	
3:00	
4:00	
5:00	
6:00	
7:00	
8:00	
9:00	
10:00	
11:00	

Sunday 21

TODAY'S GOAL

PRIORITIES

1
2
3

Time	
5:00	
6:00	
7:00	
8:00	
9:00	
10:00	
11:00	
12:00	
1:00	
2:00	
3:00	
4:00	
5:00	
6:00	
7:00	
8:00	
9:00	
10:00	
11:00	

Gratitude box

March 22-28

This week's priority

Top priority
....
....
....
....

Priority
....
....
....
....

Errands
....
....
....
....

Events | Appointments | Due dates

....
....
....
....
....
....
....
....
....
....
....

"To live your greatest life, you must first become a leader within yourself.
Take charge of your life, begin attracting and manifesting all that you
desire in life."

– Sonia Ricotti

notes | ideas

Positive Habits

	M	T	W	T	F	S	S
Gratitude							
Excercise							
Meditation							
Affirmations							

March

M	T	W	T	F	S	S
1	2	3	4	5	6	7
8	9	10	11	12	13	14
15	16	17	18	19	20	21
22	23	24	25	26	27	28
29	30	31				

April

M	T	W	T	F	S	S
			1	2	3	4
5	6	7	8	9	10	11
12	13	14	15	16	17	18
19	20	21	22	23	24	25
26	27	28	29	30		

Monday 22

TODAY'S GOAL

PRIORITIES
1
2
3

5:00
6:00
7:00
8:00
9:00
10:00
11:00
12:00
1:00
2:00
3:00
4:00
5:00
6:00
7:00
8:00
9:00
10:00
11:00

Tuesday 23

TODAY'S GOAL

PRIORITIES
1
2
3

5:00
6:00
7:00
8:00
9:00
10:00
11:00
12:00
1:00
2:00
3:00
4:00
5:00
6:00
7:00
8:00
9:00
10:00
11:00

Wednesday 24

TODAY'S GOAL

PRIORITIES
1
2
3

5:00
6:00
7:00
8:00
9:00
10:00
11:00
12:00
1:00
2:00
3:00
4:00
5:00
6:00
7:00
8:00
9:00
10:00
11:00

Thursday 25

TODAY'S GOAL

PRIORITIES
1
2
3

5:00
6:00
7:00
8:00
9:00
10:00
11:00
12:00
1:00
2:00
3:00
4:00
5:00
6:00
7:00
8:00
9:00
10:00
11:00

Friday 26

TODAY'S GOAL

PRIORITIES
1
2
3

5:00
6:00
7:00
8:00
9:00
10:00
11:00
12:00
1:00
2:00
3:00
4:00
5:00
6:00
7:00
8:00
9:00
10:00
11:00

Saturday 27

TODAY'S GOAL

PRIORITIES
1
2
3

5:00
6:00
7:00
8:00
9:00
10:00
11:00
12:00
1:00
2:00
3:00
4:00
5:00
6:00
7:00
8:00
9:00
10:00
11:00

Sunday 28

TODAY'S GOAL

PRIORITIES
1
2
3

5:00
6:00
7:00
8:00
9:00
10:00
11:00
12:00
1:00
2:00
3:00
4:00
5:00
6:00
7:00
8:00
9:00
10:00
11:00

Gratitude box

March 29-April 4

This week's priority

Top priority

....
....
....
....

Priority

....
....
....
....

Errands

....
....
....
....

Events | Appointments | Due dates

....
....
....
....
....
....
....
....
....
....
....

"Very little is needed to make a happy life; it is all within yourself,
in your way of thinking."

– Marcus Aurelius

notes | ideas

Positive Habits

	M	T	W	T	F	S	S
Gratitude							
Excercise							
Meditation							
Affirmations							

March

M	T	W	T	F	S	S
1	2	3	4	5	6	7
8	9	10	11	12	13	14
15	16	17	18	19	20	21
22	23	24	25	26	27	28
29	30	31				

April

M	T	W	T	F	S	S
			1	2	3	4
5	6	7	8	9	10	11
12	13	14	15	16	17	18
19	20	21	22	23	24	25
26	27	28	29	30		

Monday 29

TODAY'S GOAL

PRIORITIES
1
2
3

5.00
6.00
7.00
8.00
9.00
10.00
11.00
12.00
1.00
2.00
3.00
4.00
5.00
6.00
7.00
8.00
9.00
10.00
11.00

Tuesday 30

TODAY'S GOAL

PRIORITIES
1
2
3

5.00
6.00
7.00
8.00
9.00
10.00
11.00
12.00
1.00
2.00
3.00
4.00
5.00
6.00
7.00
8.00
9.00
10.00
11.00

Wednesday 31

TODAY'S GOAL

PRIORITIES
1
2
3

5.00
6.00
7.00
8.00
9.00
10.00
11.00
12.00
1.00
2.00
3.00
4.00
5.00
6.00
7.00
8.00
9.00
10.00
11.00

Thursday 1

TODAY'S GOAL

PRIORITIES
1
2
3

5.00
6.00
7.00
8.00
9.00
10.00
11.00
12.00
1.00
2.00
3.00
4.00
5.00
6.00
7.00
8.00
9.00
10.00
11.00

Friday 2

Good Friday

TODAY'S GOAL

PRIORITIES
1
2
3

5.00
6.00
7.00
8.00
9.00
10.00
11.00
12.00
1.00
2.00
3.00
4.00
5.00
6.00
7.00
8.00
9.00
10.00
11.00

Saturday 3

TODAY'S GOAL

PRIORITIES
1
2
3

5.00
6.00
7.00
8.00
9.00
10.00
11.00
12.00
1.00
2.00
3.00
4.00
5.00
6.00
7.00
8.00
9.00
10.00
11.00

Sunday 4

Easter Sunday

TODAY'S GOAL

PRIORITIES
1
2
3

5.00
6.00
7.00
8.00
9.00
10.00
11.00
12.00
1.00
2.00
3.00
4.00
5.00
6.00
7.00
8.00
9.00
10.00
11.00

Gratitude box

Reflect on your month

When you start actively observing and understanding the invisible parts of yourself – your emotions – you'll equip yourself with the tools to make visible changes in your day-to-day life. Observe how your emotions and feelings change over weeks and months. Become aware of them and change them to more positive feelings so you can attract and manifest the life of your dreams.

Check how balanced you lived your month.

What did I learn this month?

....
....
....
....

How was I feeling this month?

My top 5 achievements this month

....
....
....
....
....

Did I enjoy what I was doing this month?

....
....
....
....
....

How did I make myself feel good?

....
....
....
....
....

How do I feel about my progress this month?

_____
_____
_____
_____

What are the greatest insights that I have gained?

_____
_____
_____
_____

What mental blocks did I encounter?

_____
_____
_____
_____

What / who inspired me this month?

_____
_____
_____
_____

What actions can I take to improve?

_____
_____
_____
_____

2021

April

M	T	W	T	F	S	S
			1	2	3	4
5	6	7	8	9	10	11
12	13	14	15	16	17	18
19	20	21	22	23	24	25
26	27	28	29	30		

Monthly
Mood Tracker

Our Mood Tracker is a powerful and easy-to-use tool that allows you to track your emotions – or moods – on a regular basis.

You want to lead a fulfilling, happy life. All of that becomes so much simpler with the Mood Tracker. The perfect mental health support system, this Mood Tracker charts your triggers, looks at your ups and downs, and gives you permission to feel so you can understand your anxiety, support your stress relief, and become happier all around.

By tracking your moods, you may be able to determine situations or times that your mood goes up or down. Such situations are sometimes called triggers. For instance, if you notice you get depressed every time you visit your parents, that's important information that you can use to help you understand yourself better.

Reflect on emotions daily – gain insight into the patterns of your moods, triggers, coping skills, and mindsets.

Chart your emotions. Relieve your anxiety. BUILD A HAPPIER YOU!

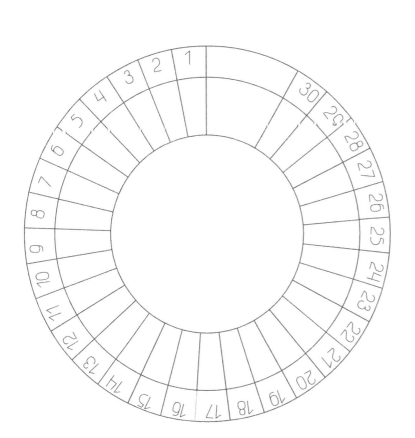

COLOR YOUR MOOD

Angry	
Annoyed	
Anxious	
Ashamed	
Confused	
Energetic	
Excited	
Exhausted	
Happy	
Sad	
Relaxed	
Productive	

Monthly Goal Planner

GOAL

REWARD

✓	ACTION STEPS	NOTES

PROGRESS TRACKER

| 25% | 50% | 75% | 100% |

NOTES

GOAL

REWARD

✓	ACTION STEPS	NOTES

PROGRESS TRACKER

| 25% | 50% | 75% | 100% |

NOTES

Monthly Habit Tracker

Monthly habit tracker can be particularly powerful on a bad day. When you're feeling down, it's easy to forget about all the progress you have already made. Habit tracking provides visual proof of your hard work – a subtle reminder of how far you've come. Plus, the empty square you see each morning can motivate you to get started because you don't want to lose your progress by breaking your streak.

COLOR   ESSENTIAL HABITS

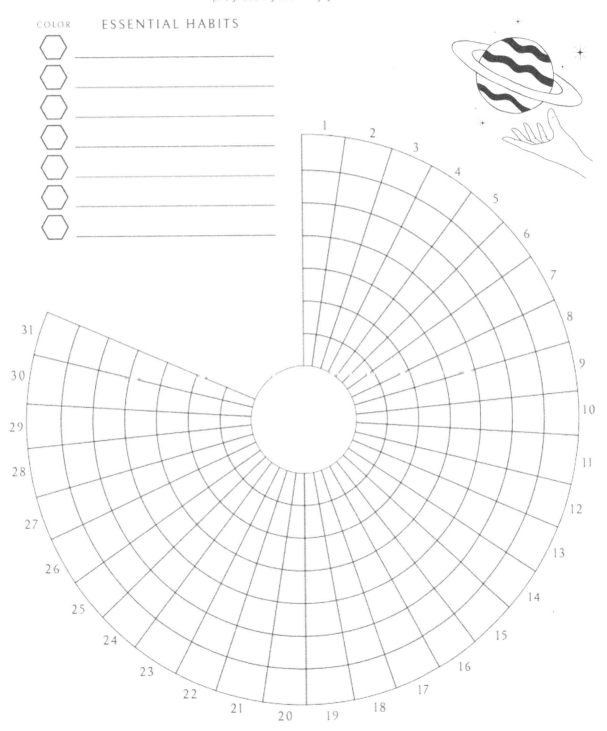

April 5-11

This week's priority

Top priority

....
....
....
....

Priority

....
....
....
....

Errands

....
....
....

Events | Appointments | Due dates

....
....
....
....
....
....
....
....
....
....
....

"Man, alone, has the power to transform his thoughts into physical reality;
man, alone, can dream and make his dreams come true."

– Napoleon Hill

notes | ideas

Positive Habits

	M	T	W	T	F	S	S
Gratitude							
Excercise							
Meditation							
Affirmations							

March

M	T	W	T	F	S	S
1	2	3	4	5	6	7
8	9	10	11	12	13	14
15	16	17	18	19	20	21
22	23	24	25	26	27	28
29	30	31				

April

M	T	W	T	F	S	S
			1	2	3	4
5	6	7	8	9	10	11
12	13	14	15	16	17	18
19	20	21	22	23	24	25
26	27	28	29	30		

Monday 5

TODAY'S GOAL

PRIORITIES

1
2
3

5:00	
6:00	
7:00	
8:00	
9:00	
10:00	
11:00	
12:00	
1:00	
2:00	
3:00	
4:00	
5:00	
6:00	
7:00	
8:00	
9:00	
10:00	
11:00	

Tuesday 6

TODAY'S GOAL

PRIORITIES

1
2
3

5:00	
6:00	
7:00	
8:00	
9:00	
10:00	
11:00	
12:00	
1:00	
2:00	
3:00	
4:00	
5:00	
6:00	
7:00	
8:00	
9:00	
10:00	
11:00	

Wednesday 7

TODAY'S GOAL

PRIORITIES

1
2
3

5:00	
6:00	
7:00	
8:00	
9:00	
10:00	
11:00	
12:00	
1:00	
2:00	
3:00	
4:00	
5:00	
6:00	
7:00	
8:00	
9:00	
10:00	
11:00	

Thursday 8

TODAY'S GOAL

PRIORITIES

1
2
3

5:00	
6:00	
7:00	
8:00	
9:00	
10:00	
11:00	
12:00	
1:00	
2:00	
3:00	
4:00	
5:00	
6:00	
7:00	
8:00	
9:00	
10:00	
11:00	

Friday 9

TODAY'S GOAL

PRIORITIES

1
2
3

5:00	
6:00	
7:00	
8:00	
9:00	
10:00	
11:00	
12:00	
1:00	
2:00	
3:00	
4:00	
5:00	
6:00	
7:00	
8:00	
9:00	
10:00	
11:00	

Saturday 10

TODAY'S GOAL

PRIORITIES

1
2
3

5:00	
6:00	
7:00	
8:00	
9:00	
10:00	
11:00	
12:00	
1:00	
2:00	
3:00	
4:00	
5:00	
6:00	
7:00	
8:00	
9:00	
10:00	
11:00	

Sunday 11

TODAY'S GOAL

PRIORITIES

1
2
3

5:00	
6:00	
7:00	
8:00	
9:00	
10:00	
11:00	
12:00	
1:00	
2:00	
3:00	
4:00	
5:00	
6:00	
7:00	
8:00	
9:00	
10:00	
11:00	

Gratitude box

April 12-18

This week's priority

Top priority

....
....
....
....

Priority

....
....
....
....

Errands

....
....
....

Events | Appointments | Due dates

....
....
....
....
....
....
....
....
....
....
....

"The idea is the first currency of the Universe, so pay attention to the ideas that are in harmony with your vision."

— Mary Morrissey

notes | ideas

Positive Habits

	M	T	W	T	F	S	S
Gratitude							
Excercise							
Meditation							
Affirmations							

March

M	T	W	T	F	S	S
1	2	3	4	5	6	7
8	9	10	11	12	13	14
15	16	17	18	19	20	21
22	23	24	25	26	27	28
29	30	31				

April

M	T	W	T	F	S	S
			1	2	3	4
5	6	7	8	9	10	11
12	13	14	15	16	17	18
19	20	21	22	23	24	25
26	27	28	29	30		

Monday 12

TODAY'S GOAL

PRIORITIES
1
2
3

5.00	
6.00	
7.00	
8.00	
9.00	
10.00	
11.00	
12.00	
1.00	
2.00	
3.00	
4.00	
5.00	
6.00	
7.00	
8.00	
9.00	
10.00	
11.00	

Tuesday 13

TODAY'S GOAL

PRIORITIES
1
2
3

5.00	
6.00	
7.00	
8.00	
9.00	
10.00	
11.00	
12.00	
1.00	
2.00	
3.00	
4.00	
5.00	
6.00	
7.00	
8.00	
9.00	
10.00	
11.00	

Wednesday 14

TODAY'S GOAL

PRIORITIES
1
2
3

5.00	
6.00	
7.00	
8.00	
9.00	
10.00	
11.00	
12.00	
1.00	
2.00	
3.00	
4.00	
5.00	
6.00	
7.00	
8.00	
9.00	
10.00	
11.00	

Thursday 15

TODAY'S GOAL

PRIORITIES
1
2
3

5.00	
6.00	
7.00	
8.00	
9.00	
10.00	
11.00	
12.00	
1.00	
2.00	
3.00	
4.00	
5.00	
6.00	
7.00	
8.00	
9.00	
10.00	
11.00	

Friday 16

TODAY'S GOAL

PRIORITIES
1
2
3

5.00	
6.00	
7.00	
8.00	
9.00	
10.00	
11.00	
12.00	
1.00	
2.00	
3.00	
4.00	
5.00	
6.00	
7.00	
8.00	
9.00	
10.00	
11.00	

Saturday 17

TODAY'S GOAL

PRIORITIES
1
2
3

5.00	
6.00	
7.00	
8.00	
9.00	
10.00	
11.00	
12.00	
1.00	
2.00	
3.00	
4.00	
5.00	
6.00	
7.00	
8.00	
9.00	
10.00	
11.00	

Sunday 18

TODAY'S GOAL

PRIORITIES
1
2
3

5.00	
6.00	
7.00	
8.00	
9.00	
10.00	
11.00	
12.00	
1.00	
2.00	
3.00	
4.00	
5.00	
6.00	
7.00	
8.00	
9.00	
10.00	
11.00	

Gratitude box

April 19-25

This week's priority

....
....
....
....

....
....
....
....

....
....
....

Events ǀ Appointments ǀ Due dates

....
....
....
....
....
....
....
....
....
....
....

"There are no limitations to the mind except those we acknowledge. Both poverty and riches are the offspring of thought!"

– Napoleon Hill

notes ǀ ideas

Positive Habits

	M	T	W	T	F	S	S
Gratitude							
Excercise							
Meditation							
Affirmations							

April

M	T	W	T	F	S	S
			1	2	3	4
5	6	7	8	9	10	11
12	13	14	15	16	17	18
19	20	21	22	23	24	25
26	27	28	29	30		

May

M	T	W	T	F	S	S
					1	2
3	4	5	6	7	8	9
10	11	12	13	14	15	16
17	18	19	20	21	22	23
24	25	26	27	28	29	30
31						

Monday 19

TODAY'S GOAL

PRIORITIES
1
2
3

5.00
6.00
7.00
8.00
9.00
10.00
11.00
12.00
1.00
2.00
3.00
4.00
5.00
6.00
7.00
8.00
9.00
10.00
11.00

Tuesday 20

TODAY'S GOAL

PRIORITIES
1
2
3

5.00
6.00
7.00
8.00
9.00
10.00
11.00
12.00
1.00
2.00
3.00
4.00
5.00
6.00
7.00
8.00
9.00
10.00
11.00

Wednesday 21

TODAY'S GOAL

PRIORITIES
1
2
3

5.00
6.00
7.00
8.00
9.00
10.00
11.00
12.00
1.00
2.00
3.00
4.00
5.00
6.00
7.00
8.00
9.00
10.00
11.00

Thursday 22

TODAY'S GOAL

PRIORITIES
1
2
3

5.00
6.00
7.00
8.00
9.00
10.00
11.00
12.00
1.00
2.00
3.00
4.00
5.00
6.00
7.00
8.00
9.00
10.00
11.00

Friday 23

TODAY'S GOAL

PRIORITIES
1
2
3

5.00
6.00
7.00
8.00
9.00
10.00
11.00
12.00
1.00
2.00
3.00
4.00
5.00
6.00
7.00
8.00
9.00
10.00
11.00

Saturday 24

TODAY'S GOAL

PRIORITIES
1
2
3

5.00
6.00
7.00
8.00
9.00
10.00
11.00
12.00
1.00
2.00
3.00
4.00
5.00
6.00
7.00
8.00
9.00
10.00
11.00

Sunday 25

TODAY'S GOAL

PRIORITIES
1
2
3

5.00
6.00
7.00
8.00
9.00
10.00
11.00
12.00
1.00
2.00
3.00
4.00
5.00
6.00
7.00
8.00
9.00
10.00
11.00

Gratitude box

April 26-May 2

This week's priority

Top priority
....
....
....
....
....

Priority
....
....
....

Errands
....
....
....

Events | Appointments | Due dates

....
....
....
....
....
....
....
....
....
....

"Everything you want is out there waiting for you to ask. Everything you
want also wants you. But you have to take action to get it."

– Jack Canfield

notes | ideas

Positive Habits

	M	T	W	T	F	S	S
Gratitude							
Excercise							
Meditation							
Affirmations							

April

M	T	W	T	F	S	S
			1	2	3	4
5	6	7	8	9	10	11
12	13	14	15	16	17	18
19	20	21	22	23	24	25
26	27	28	29	30		

May

M	T	W	T	F	S	S
					1	2
3	4	5	6	7	8	9
10	11	12	13	14	15	16
17	18	19	20	21	22	23
24	25	26	27	28	29	30
31						

Monday 26	Tuesday 27	Wednesday 28	Thursday 29

Monday 26

TODAY'S GOAL

PRIORITIES
1
2
3

5.00
6.00
7.00
8.00
9.00
10.00
11.00
12.00
1.00
2.00
3.00
4.00
5.00
6.00
7.00
8.00
9.00
10.00
11.00

Tuesday 27

TODAY'S GOAL

PRIORITIES
1
2
3

5.00
6.00
7.00
8.00
9.00
10.00
11.00
12.00
1.00
2.00
3.00
4.00
5.00
6.00
7.00
8.00
9.00
10.00
11.00

Wednesday 28

TODAY'S GOAL

PRIORITIES
1
2
3

5.00
6.00
7.00
8.00
9.00
10.00
11.00
12.00
1.00
2.00
3.00
4.00
5.00
6.00
7.00
8.00
9.00
10.00
11.00

Thursday 29

TODAY'S GOAL

PRIORITIES
1
2
3

5.00
6.00
7.00
8.00
9.00
10.00
11.00
12.00
1.00
2.00
3.00
4.00
5.00
6.00
7.00
8.00
9.00
10.00
11.00

Friday 30

TODAY'S GOAL

PRIORITIES
1
2
3

5.00
6.00
7.00
8.00
9.00
10.00
11.00
12.00
1.00
2.00
3.00
4.00
5.00
6.00
7.00
8.00
9.00
10.00
11.00

Saturday 1

TODAY'S GOAL

PRIORITIES
1
2
3

5.00
6.00
7.00
8.00
9.00
10.00
11.00
12.00
1.00
2.00
3.00
4.00
5.00
6.00
7.00
8.00
9.00
10.00
11.00

Sunday 2

TODAY'S GOAL

PRIORITIES
1
2
3

5.00
6.00
7.00
8.00
9.00
10.00
11.00
12.00
1.00
2.00
3.00
4.00
5.00
6.00
7.00
8.00
9.00
10.00
11.00

Gratitude box

Reflect on your month

When you start actively observing and understanding the invisible parts of yourself – your emotions – you'll equip yourself with the tools to make visible changes in your day-to-day life. Observe how your emotions and feelings change over weeks and months. Become aware of them and change them to more positive feelings so you can attract and manifest the life of your dreams.

Check how balanced you lived your month.

What did I learn this month?

....
....
....
....

How was I feeling this month?

My top 5 achievements this month

....
....
....
....
....

Did I enjoy what I was doing this month?

....
....
....
....
....

How did I make myself feel good?

....
....
....
....
....

How do I feel about my progress this month?

_____

_____

_____

_____

What are the greatest insights that I have gained?

_____

_____

_____

_____

What mental blocks did I encounter?

_____

_____

_____

_____

What / who inspired me this month?

_____

_____

_____

_____

What actions can I take to improve?

_____

_____

_____

_____

2021

May

M	T	W	T	F	S	S
					1	2
3	4	5	6	7	8	9
10	11	12	13	14	15	16
17	18	19	20	21	22	23
24	25	26	27	28	29	30
31						

Monthly
Mood Tracker

Our Mood Tracker is a powerful and easy-to-use tool that allows you to track your emotions – or moods – on a regular basis.

You want to lead a fulfilling, happy life. All of that becomes so much simpler with the Mood Tracker. The perfect mental health support system, this Mood Tracker charts your triggers, looks at your ups and downs, and gives you permission to feel so you can understand your anxiety, support your stress relief, and become happier all around.

By tracking your moods, you may be able to determine situations or times that your mood goes up or down. Such situations are sometimes called triggers. For instance, if you notice you get depressed every time you visit your parents, that's important information that you can use to help you understand yourself better.

Reflect on emotions daily – gain insight into the patterns of your moods, triggers, coping skills, and mindsets.

Chart your emotions. Relieve your anxiety. BUILD A HAPPIER YOU!

COLOR YOUR MOOD

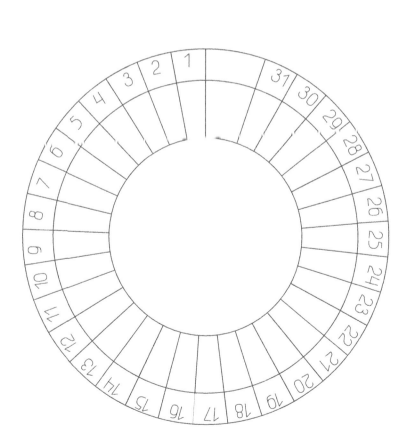

Angry	
Annoyed	
Anxious	
Ashamed	
Confused	
Energetic	
Excited	
Exhausted	
Happy	
Sad	
Relaxed	
Productive	

Monthly Goal Planner

GOAL

REWARD

⌄	ACTION STEPS	NOTES

PROGRESS TRACKER

25% 50% 75% 100%

NOTES

GOAL

REWARD

⌄	ACTION STEPS	NOTES

PROGRESS TRACKER

25% 50% 75% 100%

NOTES

Monthly Habit Tracker

Monthly habit tracker can be particularly powerful on a bad day. When you're feeling down, it's easy to forget about all the progress you have already made. Habit tracking provides visual proof of your hard work — a subtle reminder of how far you've come. Plus, the empty square you see each morning can motivate you to get started because you don't want to lose your progress by breaking your streak.

COLOR   ESSENTIAL HABITS

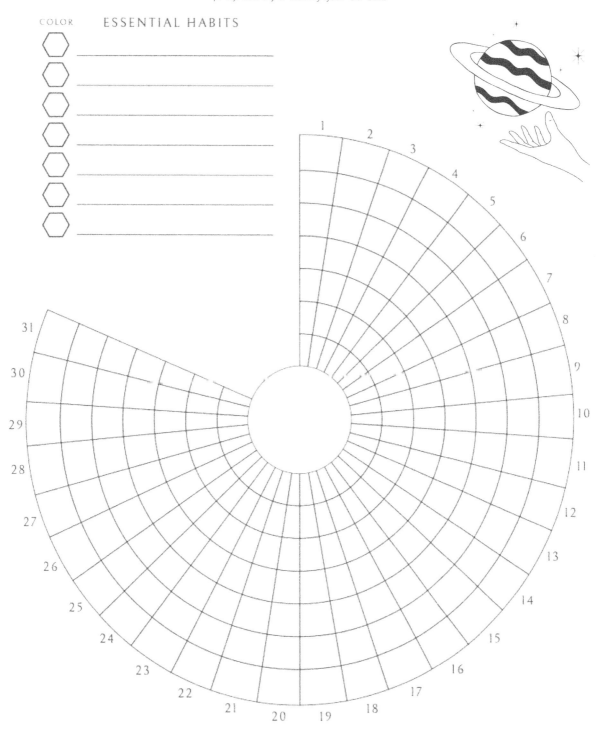

May 3-9

This week's priority

Top priority

....
....
....
....
....

Priority

....
....
....
....

Errands

....
....
....

Events | Appointments | Due dates

....
....
....
....
....
....
....
....
....
....
....

"Most people are thinking about what they don't want, and they're
wondering why it shows up over and over again."

– John Assaraf

notes | ideas

Positive Habits

	M	T	W	T	F	S	S
Gratitude							
Excercise							
Meditation							
Affirmations							

April

M	T	W	T	F	S	S
			1	2	3	4
5	6	7	8	9	10	11
12	13	14	15	16	17	18
19	20	21	22	23	24	25
26	27	28	29	30		

May

M	T	W	T	F	S	S
					1	2
3	4	5	6	7	8	9
10	11	12	13	14	15	16
17	18	19	20	21	22	23
24	25	26	27	28	29	30
31						

Monday 3

TODAY'S GOAL

PRIORITIES
1
2
3

5.00	
6.00	
7.00	
8.00	
9.00	
10.00	
11.00	
12.00	
1.00	
2.00	
3.00	
4.00	
5.00	
6.00	
7.00	
8.00	
9.00	
10.00	
11.00	

Tuesday 4

TODAY'S GOAL

PRIORITIES
1
2
3

5.00	
6.00	
7.00	
8.00	
9.00	
10.00	
11.00	
12.00	
1.00	
2.00	
3.00	
4.00	
5.00	
6.00	
7.00	
8.00	
9.00	
10.00	
11.00	

Wednesday 5

TODAY'S GOAL

PRIORITIES
1
2
3

5.00	
6.00	
7.00	
8.00	
9.00	
10.00	
11.00	
12.00	
1.00	
2.00	
3.00	
4.00	
5.00	
6.00	
7.00	
8.00	
9.00	
10.00	
11.00	

Thursday 6

TODAY'S GOAL

PRIORITIES
1
2
3

5.00	
6.00	
7.00	
8.00	
9.00	
10.00	
11.00	
12.00	
1.00	
2.00	
3.00	
4.00	
5.00	
6.00	
7.00	
8.00	
9.00	
10.00	
11.00	

Friday 7

TODAY'S GOAL

PRIORITIES
1
2
3

5.00	
6.00	
7.00	
8.00	
9.00	
10.00	
11.00	
12.00	
1.00	
2.00	
3.00	
4.00	
5.00	
6.00	
7.00	
8.00	
9.00	
10.00	
11.00	

Saturday 8

TODAY'S GOAL

PRIORITIES
1
2
3

5.00	
6.00	
7.00	
8.00	
9.00	
10.00	
11.00	
12.00	
1.00	
2.00	
3.00	
4.00	
5.00	
6.00	
7.00	
8.00	
9.00	
10.00	
11.00	

Sunday 9

Mother's Day

TODAY'S GOAL

PRIORITIES
1
2
3

5.00	
6.00	
7.00	
8.00	
9.00	
10.00	
11.00	
12.00	
1.00	
2.00	
3.00	
4.00	
5.00	
6.00	
7.00	
8.00	
9.00	
10.00	
11.00	

Gratitude box

May 10-16

This week's priority

Top priority

....
....
....

Priority

....
....
....

Errands

....
....
....

Events † Appointments † Due dates

....
....
....
....
....
....
....
....
....
....

"The first step to getting the things you want out of life is this:
Decide what you want."

– Ben Stein

notes † ideas

Positive Habits

	M	T	W	T	F	S	S
Gratitude							
Excercise							
Meditation							
Affirmations							

April

M	T	W	T	F	S	S
			1	2	3	4
5	6	7	8	9	10	11
12	13	14	15	16	17	18
19	20	21	22	23	24	25
26	27	28	29	30		

May

M	T	W	T	F	S	S
					1	2
3	4	5	6	7	8	9
10	11	12	13	14	15	16
17	18	19	20	21	22	23
24	25	26	27	28	29	30
31						

Monday 10

TODAY'S GOAL

PRIORITIES

1
2
3

5.00
6.00
7.00
8.00
9.00
10.00
11.00
12.00
1.00
2.00
3.00
4.00
5.00
6.00
7.00
8.00
9.00
10.00
11.00

Tuesday 11

TODAY'S GOAL

PRIORITIES

1
2
3

5.00
6.00
7.00
8.00
9.00
10.00
11.00
12.00
1.00
2.00
3.00
4.00
5.00
6.00
7.00
8.00
9.00
10.00
11.00

Wednesday 12

TODAY'S GOAL

PRIORITIES

1
2
3

5.00
6.00
7.00
8.00
9.00
10.00
11.00
12.00
1.00
2.00
3.00
4.00
5.00
6.00
7.00
8.00
9.00
10.00
11.00

Thursday 13

TODAY'S GOAL

PRIORITIES

1
2
3

5.00
6.00
7.00
8.00
9.00
10.00
11.00
12.00
1.00
2.00
3.00
4.00
5.00
6.00
7.00
8.00
9.00
10.00
11.00

Friday 14

TODAY'S GOAL

PRIORITIES

1
2
3

5.00
6.00
7.00
8.00
9.00
10.00
11.00
12.00
1.00
2.00
3.00
4.00
5.00
6.00
7.00
8.00
9.00
10.00
11.00

Saturday 15

TODAY'S GOAL

PRIORITIES

1
2
3

5.00
6.00
7.00
8.00
9.00
10.00
11.00
12.00
1.00
2.00
3.00
4.00
5.00
6.00
7.00
8.00
9.00
10.00
11.00

Sunday 16

TODAY'S GOAL

PRIORITIES

1
2
3

5.00
6.00
7.00
8.00
9.00
10.00
11.00
12.00
1.00
2.00
3.00
4.00
5.00
6.00
7.00
8.00
9.00
10.00
11.00

Gratitude box

May 17-23

This week's priority

Top priority

....
....
....
....
....

Priority

....
....
....
....
....

Errands

....
....
....

Events | Appointments | Due dates

....
....
....
....
....
....
....
....
....
....
....
....
....

"Think the thought until you believe it, and once you believe it, it is."

— Abraham Hicks

notes | ideas

Positive Habits

	M	T	W	T	F	S	S
Gratitude							
Excercise							
Meditation							
Affirmations							

May

M	T	W	T	F	S	S
					1	2
3	4	5	6	7	8	9
10	11	12	13	14	15	16
17	18	19	20	21	22	23
24	25	26	27	28	29	30
31						

June

M	T	W	T	F	S	S
	1	2	3	4	5	6
7	8	9	10	11	12	13
14	15	16	17	18	19	20
21	22	23	24	25	26	27
28	29	30				

Monday 17

TODAY'S GOAL

PRIORITIES

1
2
3

5:00	
6:00	
7:00	
8:00	
9:00	
10:00	
11:00	
12:00	
1:00	
2:00	
3:00	
4:00	
5:00	
6:00	
7:00	
8:00	
9:00	
10:00	
11:00	

Tuesday 18

TODAY'S GOAL

PRIORITIES

1
2
3

5:00	
6:00	
7:00	
8:00	
9:00	
10:00	
11:00	
12:00	
1:00	
2:00	
3:00	
4:00	
5:00	
6:00	
7:00	
8:00	
9:00	
10:00	
11:00	

Wednesday 19

TODAY'S GOAL

PRIORITIES

1
2
3

5:00	
6:00	
7:00	
8:00	
9:00	
10:00	
11:00	
12:00	
1:00	
2:00	
3:00	
4:00	
5:00	
6:00	
7:00	
8:00	
9:00	
10:00	
11:00	

Thursday 20

TODAY'S GOAL

PRIORITIES

1
2
3

5:00	
6:00	
7:00	
8:00	
9:00	
10:00	
11:00	
12:00	
1:00	
2:00	
3:00	
4:00	
5:00	
6:00	
7:00	
8:00	
9:00	
10:00	
11:00	

Friday 21

TODAY'S GOAL

PRIORITIES

1
2
3

5:00	
6:00	
7:00	
8:00	
9:00	
10:00	
11:00	
12:00	
1:00	
2:00	
3:00	
4:00	
5:00	
6:00	
7:00	
8:00	
9:00	
10:00	
11:00	

Saturday 22

TODAY'S GOAL

PRIORITIES

1
2
3

5:00	
6:00	
7:00	
8:00	
9:00	
10:00	
11:00	
12:00	
1:00	
2:00	
3:00	
4:00	
5:00	
6:00	
7:00	
8:00	
9:00	
10:00	
11:00	

Sunday 23

TODAY'S GOAL

PRIORITIES

1
2
3

5:00	
6:00	
7:00	
8:00	
9:00	
10:00	
11:00	
12:00	
1:00	
2:00	
3:00	
4:00	
5:00	
6:00	
7:00	
8:00	
9:00	
10:00	
11:00	

Gratitude box

May 24-30

This week's priority

Top priority

....
....
....
....

Priority

....
....
....
....

Errands

....
....
....

Events | Appointments | Due dates

....
....
....
....
....
....
....
....
....
....
....

"Your thoughts are the architects of your destiny."

– David O. McKay

notes | ideas

Positive Habits

	M	T	W	T	F	S	S
Gratitude							
Excercise							
Meditation							
Affirmations							

May

M	T	W	T	F	S	S
					1	2
3	4	5	6	7	8	9
10	11	12	13	14	15	16
17	18	19	20	21	22	23
24	25	26	27	28	29	30
31						

June

M	T	W	T	F	S	S
	1	2	3	4	5	6
7	8	9	10	11	12	13
14	15	16	17	18	19	20
21	22	23	24	25	26	27
28	29	30				

Monday 24

TODAY'S GOAL

PRIORITIES

1
2
3

5:00	
6:00	
7:00	
8:00	
9:00	
10:00	
11:00	
12:00	
1:00	
2:00	
3:00	
4:00	
5:00	
6:00	
7:00	
8:00	
9:00	
10:00	
11:00	

Tuesday 25

TODAY'S GOAL

PRIORITIES

1
2
3

5:00	
6:00	
7:00	
8:00	
9:00	
10:00	
11:00	
12:00	
1:00	
2:00	
3:00	
4:00	
5:00	
6:00	
7:00	
8:00	
9:00	
10:00	
11:00	

Wednesday 26

TODAY'S GOAL

PRIORITIES

1
2
3

5:00	
6:00	
7:00	
8:00	
9:00	
10:00	
11:00	
12:00	
1:00	
2:00	
3:00	
4:00	
5:00	
6:00	
7:00	
8:00	
9:00	
10:00	
11:00	

Thursday 27

TODAY'S GOAL

PRIORITIES

1
2
3

5:00	
6:00	
7:00	
8:00	
9:00	
10:00	
11:00	
12:00	
1:00	
2:00	
3:00	
4:00	
5:00	
6:00	
7:00	
8:00	
9:00	
10:00	
11:00	

Friday 28

TODAY'S GOAL

PRIORITIES

1
2
3

5:00	
6:00	
7:00	
8:00	
9:00	
10:00	
11:00	
12:00	
1:00	
2:00	
3:00	
4:00	
5:00	
6:00	
7:00	
8:00	
9:00	
10:00	
11:00	

Saturday 29

TODAY'S GOAL

PRIORITIES

1
2
3

5:00	
6:00	
7:00	
8:00	
9:00	
10:00	
11:00	
12:00	
1:00	
2:00	
3:00	
4:00	
5:00	
6:00	
7:00	
8:00	
9:00	
10:00	
11:00	

Sunday 30

TODAY'S GOAL

PRIORITIES

1
2
3

5:00	
6:00	
7:00	
8:00	
9:00	
10:00	
11:00	
12:00	
1:00	
2:00	
3:00	
4:00	
5:00	
6:00	
7:00	
8:00	
9:00	
10:00	
11:00	

Gratitude box

May 31–June 6

This week's priority

Top priority

....
....
....
....
....

Priority

....
....
....
....
....

Errands

....
....
....
....

Events | Appointments | Due dates

....
....
....
....
....
....
....
....
....
....
....

"Whatever you hold in your mind on a consistent basis is exactly what you will experience in your life."

– Tony Robbins

notes | ideas

Positive Habits

	M	T	W	T	F	S	S
Gratitude							
Excercise							
Meditation							
Affirmations							

May

M	T	W	T	F	S	S
					1	2
3	4	5	6	7	8	9
10	11	12	13	14	15	16
17	18	19	20	21	22	23
24	25	26	27	28	29	30
31						

June

M	T	W	T	F	S	S
	1	2	3	4	5	6
7	8	9	10	11	12	13
14	15	16	17	18	19	20
21	22	23	24	25	26	27
28	29	30				

Monday 31
Memorial Day

TODAY'S GOAL

PRIORITIES
1
2
3

5.00	
6.00	
7.00	
8.00	
9.00	
10.00	
11.00	
12.00	
1.00	
2.00	
3.00	
4.00	
5.00	
6.00	
7.00	
8.00	
9.00	
10.00	
11.00	

Tuesday 1

TODAY'S GOAL

PRIORITIES
1
2
3

5.00	
6.00	
7.00	
8.00	
9.00	
10.00	
11.00	
12.00	
1.00	
2.00	
3.00	
4.00	
5.00	
6.00	
7.00	
8.00	
9.00	
10.00	
11.00	

Wednesday 2

TODAY'S GOAL

PRIORITIES
1
2
3

5.00	
6.00	
7.00	
8.00	
9.00	
10.00	
11.00	
12.00	
1.00	
2.00	
3.00	
4.00	
5.00	
6.00	
7.00	
8.00	
9.00	
10.00	
11.00	

Thursday 3

TODAY'S GOAL

PRIORITIES
1
2
3

5.00	
6.00	
7.00	
8.00	
9.00	
10.00	
11.00	
12.00	
1.00	
2.00	
3.00	
4.00	
5.00	
6.00	
7.00	
8.00	
9.00	
10.00	
11.00	

Friday 4

TODAY'S GOAL

PRIORITIES
1
2
3

5.00	
6.00	
7.00	
8.00	
9.00	
10.00	
11.00	
12.00	
1.00	
2.00	
3.00	
4.00	
5.00	
6.00	
7.00	
8.00	
9.00	
10.00	
11.00	

Saturday 5

TODAY'S GOAL

PRIORITIES
1
2
3

5.00	
6.00	
7.00	
8.00	
9.00	
10.00	
11.00	
12.00	
1.00	
2.00	
3.00	
4.00	
5.00	
6.00	
7.00	
8.00	
9.00	
10.00	
11.00	

Sunday 6

TODAY'S GOAL

PRIORITIES
1
2
3

5.00	
6.00	
7.00	
8.00	
9.00	
10.00	
11.00	
12.00	
1.00	
2.00	
3.00	
4.00	
5.00	
6.00	
7.00	
8.00	
9.00	
10.00	
11.00	

Gratitude box

Reflect on your month

When you start actively observing and understanding the invisible parts of yourself – your emotions – you'll equip yourself with the tools to make visible changes in your day-to-day life. Observe how your emotions and feelings change over weeks and months. Become aware of them and change them to more positive feelings so you can attract and manifest the life of your dreams.

Check how balanced you lived your month.

What did I learn this month?

....
....
....
....
....

My top 5 achievements this month

....
....
....
....
....

How was I feeling this month?

Emotion wheel with inner emotions: Happy, Sad, Disgust, Anger, Fear, Surprise. Outer emotions: Optimistic, Proud, Guilty, Depressed, Lonely, Disapproval, Awful, Disappointed, Aggressive, Mad, Hurt, Scared, Humiliated, Insecure, Amazed, Excited, Confused, Peaceful.

Did I enjoy what I was doing this month?

....
....
....
....
....

How did I make myself feel good?

....
....
....
....
....

How do I feel about my progress this month?

_____
_____
_____
_____
_____

What are the greatest insights that I have gained?

_____
_____
_____
_____
_____

What mental blocks did I encounter?

_____
_____
_____
_____
_____

What / who inspired me this month?

_____
_____
_____
_____

What actions can I take to improve?

_____
_____
_____
_____
_____

M	T	W	T	F	S	S
	1	2	3	4	5	6
7	8	9	10	11	12	13
14	15	16	17	18	19	20
21	22	23	24	25	26	27
28	29	30				

Monthly
Mood Tracker

Our Mood Tracker is a powerful and easy-to-use tool that allows you to track your emotions – or moods – on a regular basis.

You want to lead a fulfilling, happy life. All of that becomes so much simpler with the Mood Tracker. The perfect mental health support system, this Mood Tracker charts your triggers, looks at your ups and downs, and gives you permission to feel so you can understand your anxiety, support your stress relief, and become happier all around.

By tracking your moods, you may be able to determine situations or times that your mood goes up or down. Such situations are sometimes called triggers. For instance, if you notice you get depressed every time you visit your parents, that's important information that you can use to help you understand yourself better.

Reflect on emotions daily – gain insight into the patterns of your moods, triggers, coping skills, and mindsets.

Chart your emotions. Relieve your anxiety. BUILD A HAPPIER YOU!

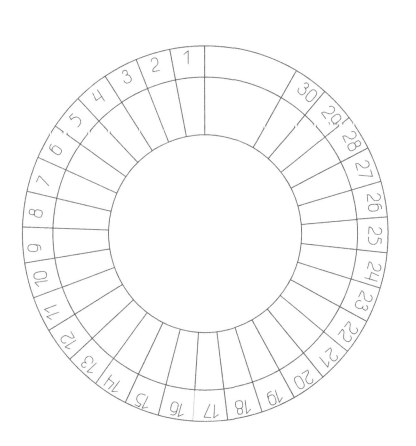

COLOR YOUR MOOD

Angry	
Annoyed	
Anxious	
Ashamed	
Confused	
Energetic	
Excited	
Exhausted	
Happy	
Sad	
Relaxed	
Productive	

Monthly Goat Planner

GOAL

REWARD

✓	ACTION STEPS	NOTES

PROGRESS TRACKER

| 25% | 50% | 75% | 100% |

NOTES

GOAL

REWARD

✓	ACTION STEPS	NOTES

PROGRESS TRACKER

| 25% | 50% | 75% | 100% |

NOTES

Monthly Habit Tracker

Monthly habit tracker can be particularly powerful on a bad day. When you're feeling down, it's easy to forget about all the progress you have already made. Habit tracking provides visual proof of your hard work – a subtle reminder of how far you've come. Plus, the empty square you see each morning can motivate you to get started because you don't want to lose your progress by breaking your streak.

COLOR   ESSENTIAL HABITS

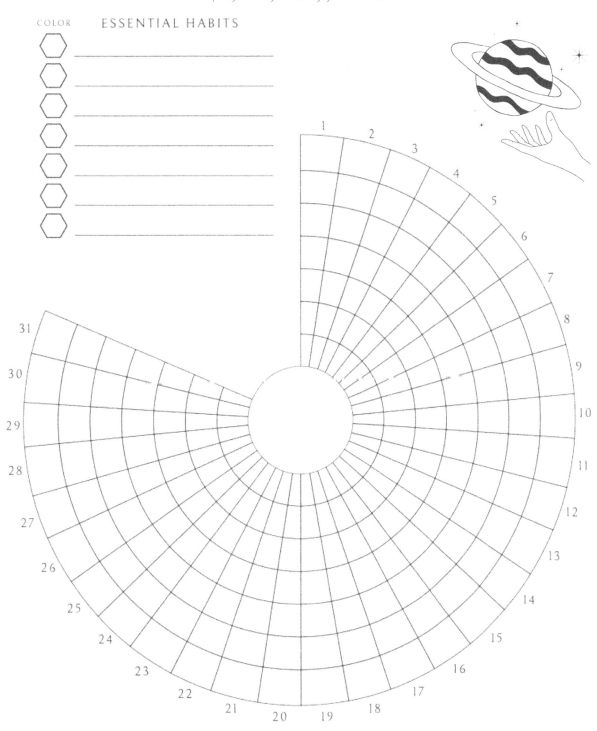

June 7-13

This week's priority

Top priority

....
....
....
....

Priority

....
....
....

Errands

....
....
....

Events | Appointments | Due dates

....
....
....
....
....
....
....
....
....
....

"Action that is inspired from aligned thoughts is joyful action."

– Abraham Hicks

notes | ideas

Positive Habits

	M	T	W	T	F	S	S
Gratitude							
Excercise							
Meditation							
Affirmations							

May

M	T	W	T	F	S	S
					1	2
3	4	5	6	7	8	9
10	11	12	13	14	15	16
17	18	19	20	21	22	23
24	25	26	27	28	29	30
31						

June

M	T	W	T	F	S	S
	1	2	3	4	5	6
7	8	9	10	11	12	13
14	15	16	17	18	19	20
21	22	23	24	25	26	27
28	29	30				

Monday 7

TODAY'S GOAL

PRIORITIES
1
2
3

5:00	
6:00	
7:00	
8:00	
9:00	
10:00	
11:00	
12:00	
1:00	
2:00	
3:00	
4:00	
5:00	
6:00	
7:00	
8:00	
9:00	
10:00	
11:00	

Tuesday 8

TODAY'S GOAL

PRIORITIES
1
2
3

5:00	
6:00	
7:00	
8:00	
9:00	
10:00	
11:00	
12:00	
1:00	
2:00	
3:00	
4:00	
5:00	
6:00	
7:00	
8:00	
9:00	
10:00	
11:00	

Wednesday 9

TODAY'S GOAL

PRIORITIES
1
2
3

5:00	
6:00	
7:00	
8:00	
9:00	
10:00	
11:00	
12:00	
1:00	
2:00	
3:00	
4:00	
5:00	
6:00	
7:00	
8:00	
9:00	
10:00	
11:00	

Thursday 10

TODAY'S GOAL

PRIORITIES
1
2
3

5:00	
6:00	
7:00	
8:00	
9:00	
10:00	
11:00	
12:00	
1:00	
2:00	
3:00	
4:00	
5:00	
6:00	
7:00	
8:00	
9:00	
10:00	
11:00	

Friday 11

TODAY'S GOAL

PRIORITIES
1
2
3

5:00	
6:00	
7:00	
8:00	
9:00	
10:00	
11:00	
12:00	
1:00	
2:00	
3:00	
4:00	
5:00	
6:00	
7:00	
8:00	
9:00	
10:00	
11:00	

Saturday 12

TODAY'S GOAL

PRIORITIES
1
2
3

5:00	
6:00	
7:00	
8:00	
9:00	
10:00	
11:00	
12:00	
1:00	
2:00	
3:00	
4:00	
5:00	
6:00	
7:00	
8:00	
9:00	
10:00	
11:00	

Sunday 13

TODAY'S GOAL

PRIORITIES
1
2
3

5:00	
6:00	
7:00	
8:00	
9:00	
10:00	
11:00	
12:00	
1:00	
2:00	
3:00	
4:00	
5:00	
6:00	
7:00	
8:00	
9:00	
10:00	
11:00	

Gratitude box

June 14-20

This week's priority

Top priority

....
....
....
....

Priority

....
....
....
....

Errands

....
....
....
....

Events | Appointments | Due dates

....
....
....
....
....
....
....
....
....
....
....

"We receive exactly what we expect to receive."

– John Holland

notes | ideas

Positive Habits

	M	T	W	T	F	S	S
Gratitude							
Excercise							
Meditation							
Affirmations							

May

M	T	W	T	F	S	S
					1	2
3	4	5	6	7	8	9
10	11	12	13	14	15	16
17	18	19	20	21	22	23
24	25	26	27	28	29	30
31						

June

M	T	W	T	F	S	S
1	2	3	4	5	6
7	8	9	10	11	12	13
14	15	16	17	18	19	20
21	22	23	24	25	26	27
28	29	30				

Monday 14

TODAY'S GOAL

PRIORITIES

1
2
3

5.00	
6.00	
7.00	
8.00	
9.00	
10.00	
11.00	
12.00	
1.00	
2.00	
3.00	
4.00	
5.00	
6.00	
7.00	
8.00	
9.00	
10.00	
11.00	

Tuesday 15

TODAY'S GOAL

PRIORITIES

1
2
3

5.00	
6.00	
7.00	
8.00	
9.00	
10.00	
11.00	
12.00	
1.00	
2.00	
3.00	
4.00	
5.00	
6.00	
7.00	
8.00	
9.00	
10.00	
11.00	

Wednesday 16

TODAY'S GOAL

PRIORITIES

1
2
3

5.00	
6.00	
7.00	
8.00	
9.00	
10.00	
11.00	
12.00	
1.00	
2.00	
3.00	
4.00	
5.00	
6.00	
7.00	
8.00	
9.00	
10.00	
11.00	

Thursday 17

TODAY'S GOAL

PRIORITIES

1
2
3

5.00	
6.00	
7.00	
8.00	
9.00	
10.00	
11.00	
12.00	
1.00	
2.00	
3.00	
4.00	
5.00	
6.00	
7.00	
8.00	
9.00	
10.00	
11.00	

Friday 18

TODAY'S GOAL

PRIORITIES

1
2
3

5.00	
6.00	
7.00	
8.00	
9.00	
10.00	
11.00	
12.00	
1.00	
2.00	
3.00	
4.00	
5.00	
6.00	
7.00	
8.00	
9.00	
10.00	
11.00	

Saturday 19

TODAY'S GOAL

PRIORITIES

1
2
3

5.00	
6.00	
7.00	
8.00	
9.00	
10.00	
11.00	
12.00	
1.00	
2.00	
3.00	
4.00	
5.00	
6.00	
7.00	
8.00	
9.00	
10.00	
11.00	

Sunday 20

Father's Day

TODAY'S GOAL

PRIORITIES

1
2
3

5.00	
6.00	
7.00	
8.00	
9.00	
10.00	
11.00	
12.00	
1.00	
2.00	
3.00	
4.00	
5.00	
6.00	
7.00	
8.00	
9.00	
10.00	
11.00	

Gratitude box

June 21-27

This week's priority

Top priority

....
....
....
....
....

Priority

....
....
....
....

Errands

....
....
....

Events † Appointments † Due dates

....
....
....
....
....
....
....
....
....
....

"We are like magnets — like attracts like. You become and attract what you think."

— Anonymous

notes † ideas

Positive Habits

	M	T	W	T	F	S	S
Gratitude							
Excercise							
Meditation							
Affirmations							

June

M	T	W	T	F	S	S
	1	2	3	4	5	6
7	8	9	10	11	12	13
14	15	16	17	18	19	20
21	22	23	24	25	26	27
28	29	30				

July

M	T	W	T	F	S	S
		1	2	3	4
5	6	7	8	9	10	11
12	13	14	15	16	17	18
19	20	21	22	23	24	25
26	27	28	29	30	31	

Monday 21

TODAY'S GOAL

PRIORITIES
1
2
3

Time	
5:00	
6:00	
7:00	
8:00	
9:00	
10:00	
11:00	
12:00	
1:00	
2:00	
3:00	
4:00	
5:00	
6:00	
7:00	
8:00	
9:00	
10:00	
11:00	

Tuesday 22

TODAY'S GOAL

PRIORITIES
1
2
3

Time	
5:00	
6:00	
7:00	
8:00	
9:00	
10:00	
11:00	
12:00	
1:00	
2:00	
3:00	
4:00	
5:00	
6:00	
7:00	
8:00	
9:00	
10:00	
11:00	

Wednesday 23

TODAY'S GOAL

PRIORITIES
1
2
3

Time	
5:00	
6:00	
7:00	
8:00	
9:00	
10:00	
11:00	
12:00	
1:00	
2:00	
3:00	
4:00	
5:00	
6:00	
7:00	
8:00	
9:00	
10:00	
11:00	

Thursday 24

TODAY'S GOAL

PRIORITIES
1
2
3

Time	
5:00	
6:00	
7:00	
8:00	
9:00	
10:00	
11:00	
12:00	
1:00	
2:00	
3:00	
4:00	
5:00	
6:00	
7:00	
8:00	
9:00	
10:00	
11:00	

Friday 25

TODAY'S GOAL

PRIORITIES
1
2
3

Time	
5:00	
6:00	
7:00	
8:00	
9:00	
10:00	
11:00	
12:00	
1:00	
2:00	
3:00	
4:00	
5:00	
6:00	
7:00	
8:00	
9:00	
10:00	
11:00	

Saturday 26

TODAY'S GOAL

PRIORITIES
1
2
3

Time	
5:00	
6:00	
7:00	
8:00	
9:00	
10:00	
11:00	
12:00	
1:00	
2:00	
3:00	
4:00	
5:00	
6:00	
7:00	
8:00	
9:00	
10:00	
11:00	

Sunday 27

TODAY'S GOAL

PRIORITIES
1
2
3

Time	
5:00	
6:00	
7:00	
8:00	
9:00	
10:00	
11:00	
12:00	
1:00	
2:00	
3:00	
4:00	
5:00	
6:00	
7:00	
8:00	
9:00	
10:00	
11:00	

Gratitude box

June 28–July 4

This week's priority

Top priority

....
....
....
....

Priority

....
....
....
....

Errands

....
....

Events | Appointments | Due dates

....
....
....
....
....
....
....
....
....
....
....

"Imagination is everything. It is the preview of life's coming attractions."

– Albert Einstein

notes | ideas

Positive Habits

	M	T	W	T	F	S	S
Gratitude							
Excercise							
Meditation							
Affirmations							

June

M	T	W	T	F	S	S
	1	2	3	4	5	6
7	8	9	10	11	12	13
14	15	16	17	18	19	20
21	22	23	24	25	26	27
28	29	30				

July

M	T	W	T	F	S	S
		1	2	3	4
5	6	7	8	9	10	11
12	13	14	15	16	17	18
19	20	21	22	23	24	25
26	27	28	29	30	31	

Monday 28

TODAY'S GOAL

PRIORITIES
1
2
3

5:00	
6:00	
7:00	
8:00	
9:00	
10:00	
11:00	
12:00	
1:00	
2:00	
3:00	
4:00	
5:00	
6:00	
7:00	
8:00	
9:00	
10:00	
11:00	

Tuesday 29

TODAY'S GOAL

PRIORITIES
1
2
3

5:00	
6:00	
7:00	
8:00	
9:00	
10:00	
11:00	
12:00	
1:00	
2:00	
3:00	
4:00	
5:00	
6:00	
7:00	
8:00	
9:00	
10:00	
11:00	

Wednesday 30

TODAY'S GOAL

PRIORITIES
1
2
3

5:00	
6:00	
7:00	
8:00	
9:00	
10:00	
11:00	
12:00	
1:00	
2:00	
3:00	
4:00	
5:00	
6:00	
7:00	
8:00	
9:00	
10:00	
11:00	

Thursday 1

TODAY'S GOAL

PRIORITIES
1
2
3

5:00	
6:00	
7:00	
8:00	
9:00	
10:00	
11:00	
12:00	
1:00	
2:00	
3:00	
4:00	
5:00	
6:00	
7:00	
8:00	
9:00	
10:00	
11:00	

Friday 2

TODAY'S GOAL

PRIORITIES
1
2
3

5:00	
6:00	
7:00	
8:00	
9:00	
10:00	
11:00	
12:00	
1:00	
2:00	
3:00	
4:00	
5:00	
6:00	
7:00	
8:00	
9:00	
10:00	
11:00	

Saturday 3

TODAY'S GOAL

PRIORITIES
1
2
3

5:00	
6:00	
7:00	
8:00	
9:00	
10:00	
11:00	
12:00	
1:00	
2:00	
3:00	
4:00	
5:00	
6:00	
7:00	
8:00	
9:00	
10:00	
11:00	

Sunday 4

Independence Day

TODAY'S GOAL

PRIORITIES
1
2
3

5:00	
6:00	
7:00	
8:00	
9:00	
10:00	
11:00	
12:00	
1:00	
2:00	
3:00	
4:00	
5:00	
6:00	
7:00	
8:00	
9:00	
10:00	
11:00	

Gratitude box

Reflect on your month

When you start actively observing and understanding the invisible parts of yourself – your emotions – you'll equip yourself with the tools to make visible changes in your day-to-day life. Observe how your emotions and feelings change over weeks and months. Become aware of them and change them to more positive feelings so you can attract and manifest the life of your dreams.

Check how balanced you lived your month.

What did I learn this month?

....
....
....
....
....

My top 5 achievements this month

....
....
....
....
....

How was I feeling this month?

Optimistic, Proud, Guilty, Depressed, Peaceful, Lonely, Confused, Disapproval, Happy, Sad, Excited, Surprise, Disgust, Awful, Amazed, Fear, Anger, Disappointed, Insecure, Aggressive, Humiliated, Scared, Hurt, Mad

Did I enjoy what I was doing this month?

....
....
....
....
....

How did I make myself feel good?

....
....
....
....
....

How do I feel about my progress this month?

_____
_____
_____
_____
_____

What are the greatest insights that I have gained?

_____
_____
_____
_____
_____

What mental blocks did I encounter?

_____
_____
_____
_____
_____

What / who inspired me this month?

_____
_____
_____
_____
_____

What actions can I take to improve?

_____
_____
_____
_____
_____

M	T	W	T	F	S	S
			1	2	3	4
5	6	7	8	9	10	11
12	13	14	15	16	17	18
19	20	21	22	23	24	25
26	27	28	29	30	31	

Monthly Mood Tracker

Our Mood Tracker is a powerful and easy-to-use tool that allows you to track your emotions – or moods – on a regular basis.

You want to lead a fulfilling, happy life. All of that becomes so much simpler with the Mood Tracker. The perfect mental health support system, this Mood Tracker charts your triggers, looks at your ups and downs, and gives you permission to feel so you can understand your anxiety, support your stress relief, and become happier all around.

By tracking your moods, you may be able to determine situations or times that your mood goes up or down. Such situations are sometimes called triggers. For instance, if you notice you get depressed every time you visit your parents, that's important information that you can use to help you understand yourself better.

Reflect on emotions daily – gain insight into the patterns of your moods, triggers, coping skills, and mindsets.

Chart your emotions. Relieve your anxiety. BUILD A HAPPIER YOU!

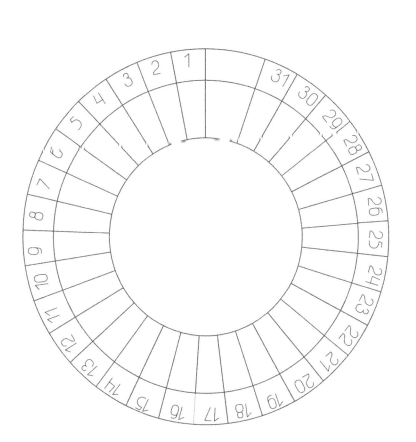

COLOR YOUR MOOD

Angry	
Annoyed	
Anxious	
Ashamed	
Confused	
Energetic	
Excited	
Exhausted	
Happy	
Sad	
Relaxed	
Productive	

Monthly Goal Planner

GOAL

REWARD

⌄	ACTION STEPS	NOTES

PROGRESS TRACKER

25%   50%   75%   100%

NOTES

GOAL

REWARD

⌄	ACTION STEPS	NOTES

PROGRESS TRACKER

25%   50%   75%   100%

NOTES

Monthly Habit Tracker

Monthly habit tracker can be particularly powerful on a bad day. When you're feeling down, it's easy to forget about all the progress you have already made. Habit tracking provides visual proof of your hard work — a subtle reminder of how far you've come. Plus, the empty square you see each morning can motivate you to get started because you don't want to lose your progress by breaking your streak.

COLOR   ESSENTIAL HABITS

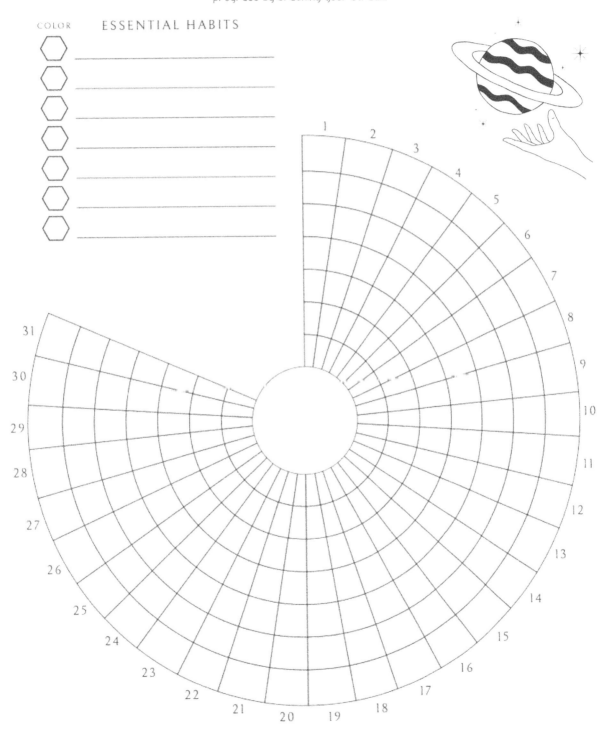

July 5-11

This week's priority

Top priority

....
....
....
....
....

Priority

....
....
....
....

Errands

....
....
....

Events | Appointments | Due dates

....
....
....
....
....
....
....
....
....
....
....
....

"When you visualize, then you materialize. If you've been there in the mind, you'll go there in the body."

– Dr. Denis Waitley

notes | ideas

Positive Habits

	M	T	W	T	F	S	S
Gratitude							
Excercise							
Meditation							
Affirmations							

June

M	T	W	T	F	S	S
	1	2	3	4	5	6
7	8	9	10	11	12	13
14	15	16	17	18	19	20
21	22	23	24	25	26	27
28	29	30				

July

M	T	W	T	F	S	S
		1	2	3	4
5	6	7	8	9	10	11
12	13	14	15	16	17	18
19	20	21	22	23	24	25
26	27	28	29	30	31	

Monday 5

TODAY'S GOAL

PRIORITIES

1
2
3

5.00
6.00
7.00
8.00
9.00
10.00
11.00
12.00
1.00
2.00
3.00
4.00
5.00
6.00
7.00
8.00
9.00
10.00
11.00

Tuesday 6

TODAY'S GOAL

PRIORITIES

1
2
3

5.00
6.00
7.00
8.00
9.00
10.00
11.00
12.00
1.00
2.00
3.00
4.00
5.00
6.00
7.00
8.00
9.00
10.00
11.00

Wednesday 7

TODAY'S GOAL

PRIORITIES

1
2
3

5.00
6.00
7.00
8.00
9.00
10.00
11.00
12.00
1.00
2.00
3.00
4.00
5.00
6.00
7.00
8.00
9.00
10.00
11.00

Thursday 8

TODAY'S GOAL

PRIORITIES

1
2
3

5.00
6.00
7.00
8.00
9.00
10.00
11.00
12.00
1.00
2.00
3.00
4.00
5.00
6.00
7.00
8.00
9.00
10.00
11.00

Friday 9

TODAY'S GOAL

PRIORITIES

1
2
3

5.00
6.00
7.00
8.00
9.00
10.00
11.00
12.00
1.00
2.00
3.00
4.00
5.00
6.00
7.00
8.00
9.00
10.00
11.00

Saturday 10

TODAY'S GOAL

PRIORITIES

1
2
3

5.00
6.00
7.00
8.00
9.00
10.00
11.00
12.00
1.00
2.00
3.00
4.00
5.00
6.00
7.00
8.00
9.00
10.00
11.00

Sunday 11

TODAY'S GOAL

PRIORITIES

1
2
3

5.00
6.00
7.00
8.00
9.00
10.00
11.00
12.00
1.00
2.00
3.00
4.00
5.00
6.00
7.00
8.00
9.00
10.00
11.00

Gratitude box

July 12-18

This week's priority

Top priority

....
....
....
....
....
....

Priority

....
....
....
....

Errands

....
....
....

Events | Appointments | Due dates

....
....
....
....
....
....
....
....
....
....
....
....

"The only person you are destined to become is... the person
you decide to be."

– Ralph Waldo Emerson"

Positive Habits

	M	T	W	T	F	S	S
Gratitude							
Excercise							
Meditation							
Affirmations							

notes | ideas

June

M	T	W	T	F	S	S
	1	2	3	4	5	6
7	8	9	10	11	12	13
14	15	16	17	18	19	20
21	22	23	24	25	26	27
28	29	30				

July

M	T	W	T	F	S	S
			1	2	3	4
5	6	7	8	9	10	11
12	13	14	15	16	17	18
19	20	21	22	23	24	25
26	27	28	29	30	31	

Monday 12

TODAY'S GOAL

PRIORITIES

1
2
3

5:00
6:00
7:00
8:00
9:00
10:00
11:00
12:00
1:00
2:00
3:00
4:00
5:00
6:00
7:00
8:00
9:00
10:00
11:00

Tuesday 13

TODAY'S GOAL

PRIORITIES

1
2
3

5:00
6:00
7:00
8:00
9:00
10:00
11:00
12:00
1:00
2:00
3:00
4:00
5:00
6:00
7:00
8:00
9:00
10:00
11:00

Wednesday 14

TODAY'S GOAL

PRIORITIES

1
2
3

5:00
6:00
7:00
8:00
9:00
10:00
11:00
12:00
1:00
2:00
3:00
4:00
5:00
6:00
7:00
8:00
9:00
10:00
11:00

Thursday 15

TODAY'S GOAL

PRIORITIES

1
2
3

5:00
6:00
7:00
8:00
9:00
10:00
11:00
12:00
1:00
2:00
3:00
4:00
5:00
6:00
7:00
8:00
9:00
10:00
11:00

Friday 16

TODAY'S GOAL

PRIORITIES

1
2
3

5:00
6:00
7:00
8:00
9:00
10:00
11:00
12:00
1:00
2:00
3:00
4:00
5:00
6:00
7:00
8:00
9:00
10:00
11:00

Saturday 17

TODAY'S GOAL

PRIORITIES

1
2
3

5:00
6:00
7:00
8:00
9:00
10:00
11:00
12:00
1:00
2:00
3:00
4:00
5:00
6:00
7:00
8:00
9:00
10:00
11:00

Sunday 18

TODAY'S GOAL

PRIORITIES

1
2
3

5:00
6:00
7:00
8:00
9:00
10:00
11:00
12:00
1:00
2:00
3:00
4:00
5:00
6:00
7:00
8:00
9:00
10:00
11:00

Gratitude box

July 19-25

This week's priority

Top priority

....
....
....
....
....

Priority

....
....
....
....

Errands

....
....
....

Events ‖ Appointments ‖ Due dates

....
....
....
....
....
....
....
....
....
....
....
....
....

"Whatever is going on in your mind, you are attracting to you."

– Bob Proctor

notes ‖ ideas

Positive Habits

	M	T	W	T	F	S	S
Gratitude							
Excercise							
Meditation							
Affirmations							

July

M	T	W	T	F	S	S
			1	2	3	4
5	6	7	8	9	10	11
12	13	14	15	16	17	18
19	20	21	22	23	24	25
26	27	28	29	30	31	

August

M	T	W	T	F	S	S
						1
2	3	4	5	6	7	8
9	10	11	12	13	14	15
16	17	18	19	20	21	22
23	24	25	26	27	28	29
30	31					

Monday 19

TODAY'S GOAL

PRIORITIES

1
2
3

5:00	
6:00	
7:00	
8:00	
9:00	
10:00	
11:00	
12:00	
1:00	
2:00	
3:00	
4:00	
5:00	
6:00	
7:00	
8:00	
9:00	
10:00	
11:00	

Tuesday 20

TODAY'S GOAL

PRIORITIES

1
2
3

5:00	
6:00	
7:00	
8:00	
9:00	
10:00	
11:00	
12:00	
1:00	
2:00	
3:00	
4:00	
5:00	
6:00	
7:00	
8:00	
9:00	
10:00	
11:00	

Wednesday 21

TODAY'S GOAL

PRIORITIES

1
2
3

5:00	
6:00	
7:00	
8:00	
9:00	
10:00	
11:00	
12:00	
1:00	
2:00	
3:00	
4:00	
5:00	
6:00	
7:00	
8:00	
9:00	
10:00	
11:00	

Thursday 22

TODAY'S GOAL

PRIORITIES

1
2
3

5:00	
6:00	
7:00	
8:00	
9:00	
10:00	
11:00	
12:00	
1:00	
2:00	
3:00	
4:00	
5:00	
6:00	
7:00	
8:00	
9:00	
10:00	
11:00	

Friday 23

TODAY'S GOAL

PRIORITIES

1
2
3

5:00	
6:00	
7:00	
8:00	
9:00	
10:00	
11:00	
12:00	
1:00	
2:00	
3:00	
4:00	
5:00	
6:00	
7:00	
8:00	
9:00	
10:00	
11:00	

Saturday 24

TODAY'S GOAL

PRIORITIES

1
2
3

5:00	
6:00	
7:00	
8:00	
9:00	
10:00	
11:00	
12:00	
1:00	
2:00	
3:00	
4:00	
5:00	
6:00	
7:00	
8:00	
9:00	
10:00	
11:00	

Sunday 25

TODAY'S GOAL

PRIORITIES

1
2
3

5:00	
6:00	
7:00	
8:00	
9:00	
10:00	
11:00	
12:00	
1:00	
2:00	
3:00	
4:00	
5:00	
6:00	
7:00	
8:00	
9:00	
10:00	
11:00	

Gratitude box

July 26-August 1

This week's priority

Top priority
....
....
....
....
....

Priority
....
....
....
....
....

Errands
....
....
....
....

Events | Appointments | Due dates

....
....
....
....
....
....
....
....
....
....
....
....
....

"You want to become aware of your thoughts, you want to choose
your thoughts carefully and you want to have fun with this,
because you are the masterpiece of your own life."

— Joe Vitale

notes | ideas

Positive Habits

	M	T	W	T	F	S	S
Gratitude							
Excercise							
Meditation							
Affirmations							

July

M	T	W	T	F	S	S
			1	2	3	4
5	6	7	8	9	10	11
12	13	14	15	16	17	18
19	20	21	22	23	24	25
26	27	28	29	30	31	

August

M	T	W	T	F	S	S
						1
2	3	4	5	6	7	8
9	10	11	12	13	14	15
16	17	18	19	20	21	22
23	24	25	26	27	28	29
30	31					

Monday 26

TODAY'S GOAL

PRIORITIES

1
2
3

5:00	
6:00	
7:00	
8:00	
9:00	
10:00	
11:00	
12:00	
1:00	
2:00	
3:00	
4:00	
5:00	
6:00	
7:00	
8:00	
9:00	
10:00	
11:00	

Tuesday 27

TODAY'S GOAL

PRIORITIES

1
2
3

5:00	
6:00	
7:00	
8:00	
9:00	
10:00	
11:00	
12:00	
1:00	
2:00	
3:00	
4:00	
5:00	
6:00	
7:00	
8:00	
9:00	
10:00	
11:00	

Wednesday 28

TODAY'S GOAL

PRIORITIES

1
2
3

5:00	
6:00	
7:00	
8:00	
9:00	
10:00	
11:00	
12:00	
1:00	
2:00	
3:00	
4:00	
5:00	
6:00	
7:00	
8:00	
9:00	
10:00	
11:00	

Thursday 29

TODAY'S GOAL

PRIORITIES

1
2
3

5:00	
6:00	
7:00	
8:00	
9:00	
10:00	
11:00	
12:00	
1:00	
2:00	
3:00	
4:00	
5:00	
6:00	
7:00	
8:00	
9:00	
10:00	
11:00	

Friday 30

TODAY'S GOAL

PRIORITIES

1
2
3

5:00	
6:00	
7:00	
8:00	
9:00	
10:00	
11:00	
12:00	
1:00	
2:00	
3:00	
4:00	
5:00	
6:00	
7:00	
8:00	
9:00	
10:00	
11:00	

Saturday 31

TODAY'S GOAL

PRIORITIES

1
2
3

5:00	
6:00	
7:00	
8:00	
9:00	
10:00	
11:00	
12:00	
1:00	
2:00	
3:00	
4:00	
5:00	
6:00	
7:00	
8:00	
9:00	
10:00	
11:00	

Sunday 1

TODAY'S GOAL

PRIORITIES

1
2
3

5:00	
6:00	
7:00	
8:00	
9:00	
10:00	
11:00	
12:00	
1:00	
2:00	
3:00	
4:00	
5:00	
6:00	
7:00	
8:00	
9:00	
10:00	
11:00	

Gratitude box

Reflect on your month

When you start actively observing and understanding the invisible parts of yourself – your emotions – you'll equip yourself with the tools to make visible changes in your day-to-day life. Observe how your emotions and feelings change over weeks and months. Become aware of them and change them to more positive feelings so you can attract and manifest the life of your dreams.

Check how balanced you lived your month.

What did I learn this month?

....

....

....

....

....

My top 5 achievements this month

....

....

....

....

....

How was I feeling this month?

Optimistic · Proud · Guilty · Depressed · Lonely · Disapproval · Awful · Disappointed · Aggressive · Mad · Hurt · Scared · Humiliated · Insecure · Amazed · Excited · Confused · Peaceful

Happy · Sad · Surprise · Disgust · Fear · Anger

Did I enjoy what I was doing this month?

....

....

....

....

....

How did I make myself feel good?

....

....

....

....

....

How do I feel about my progress this month?

_____
_____
_____
_____
_____

What are the greatest insights that I have gained?

_____
_____
_____
_____
_____

What mental blocks did I encounter?

_____
_____
_____
_____
_____

What / who inspired me this month?

_____
_____
_____
_____
_____

What actions can I take to improve?

_____
_____
_____
_____
_____

2021

August

M	T	W	T	F	S	S
						1
2	3	4	5	6	7	8
9	10	11	12	13	14	15
16	17	18	19	20	21	22
23	24	25	26	27	28	29
30	31					

Monthly
Mood Tracker

Our Mood Tracker is a powerful and easy-to-use tool that allows you to track your emotions – or moods – on a regular basis.

You want to lead a fulfilling, happy life. All of that becomes so much simpler with the Mood Tracker. The perfect mental health support system, this Mood Tracker charts your triggers, looks at your ups and downs, and gives you permission to feel so you can understand your anxiety, support your stress relief, and become happier all around.

By tracking your moods, you may be able to determine situations or times that your mood goes up or down. Such situations are sometimes called triggers. For instance, if you notice you get depressed every time you visit your parents, that's important information that you can use to help you understand yourself better.

Reflect on emotions daily – gain insight into the patterns of your moods, triggers, coping skills, and mindsets.

Chart your emotions. Relieve your anxiety. BUILD A HAPPIER YOU!

COLOR YOUR MOOD

Angry	
Annoyed	
Anxious	
Ashamed	
Confused	
Energetic	
Excited	
Exhausted	
Happy	
Sad	
Relaxed	
Productive	

Monthly Goal Planner

GOAL

REWARD

✓	ACTION STEPS	NOTES

PROGRESS TRACKER

25%　　　　　50%　　　　　75%　　　　　100%

NOTES

GOAL

REWARD

✓	ACTION STEPS	NOTES

PROGRESS TRACKER

25%　　　　　50%　　　　　75%　　　　　100%

NOTES

Monthly Habit Tracker

Monthly habit tracker can be particularly powerful on a bad day. When you're feeling down, it's easy to forget about all the progress you have already made. Habit tracking provides visual proof of your hard work – a subtle reminder of how far you've come. Plus, the empty square you see each morning can motivate you to get started because you don't want to lose your progress by breaking your streak.

COLOR   ESSENTIAL HABITS

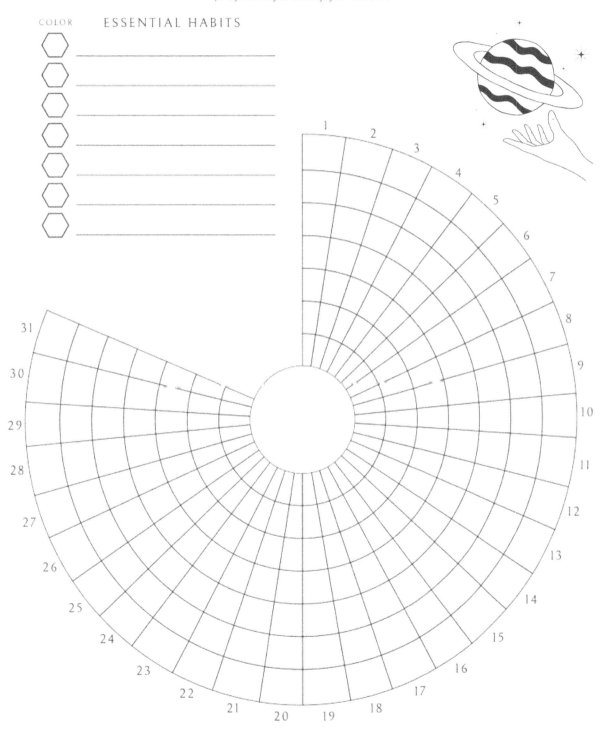

August 2-8

This week's priority

Top priority

....
....
....
....

Priority

....
....
....
....

Errands

....
....
....

Events | Appointments | Due dates

....
....
....
....
....
....
....

" You are the master of your destiny. You can influence, direct and control your own environment. You can make your life what you want it to be."

— Napoleon Hill

notes | ideas

Positive Habits

	M	T	W	T	F	S	S
Gratitude							
Excercise							
Meditation							
Affirmations							

July

M	T	W	T	F	S	S
			1	2	3	4
5	6	7	8	9	10	11
12	13	14	15	16	17	18
19	20	21	22	23	24	25
26	27	28	29	30	31	

August

M	T	W	T	F	S	S
						1
2	3	4	5	6	7	8
9	10	11	12	13	14	15
16	17	18	19	20	21	22
23	24	25	26	27	28	29
30	31					

Monday 2

TODAY'S GOAL

PRIORITIES
1
2
3

| 5:00 |
| 6:00 |
| 7:00 |
| 8:00 |
| 9:00 |
| 10:00 |
| 11:00 |
| 12:00 |
| 1:00 |
| 2:00 |
| 3:00 |
| 4:00 |
| 5:00 |
| 6:00 |
| 7:00 |
| 8:00 |
| 9:00 |
| 10:00 |
| 11:00 |

Tuesday 3

TODAY'S GOAL

PRIORITIES
1
2
3

| 5:00 |
| 6:00 |
| 7:00 |
| 8:00 |
| 9:00 |
| 10:00 |
| 11:00 |
| 12:00 |
| 1:00 |
| 2:00 |
| 3:00 |
| 4:00 |
| 5:00 |
| 6:00 |
| 7:00 |
| 8:00 |
| 9:00 |
| 10:00 |
| 11:00 |

Wednesday 4

TODAY'S GOAL

PRIORITIES
1
2
3

| 5:00 |
| 6:00 |
| 7:00 |
| 8:00 |
| 9:00 |
| 10:00 |
| 11:00 |
| 12:00 |
| 1:00 |
| 2:00 |
| 3:00 |
| 4:00 |
| 5:00 |
| 6:00 |
| 7:00 |
| 8:00 |
| 9:00 |
| 10:00 |
| 11:00 |

Thursday 5

TODAY'S GOAL

PRIORITIES
1
2
3

| 5:00 |
| 6:00 |
| 7:00 |
| 8:00 |
| 9:00 |
| 10:00 |
| 11:00 |
| 12:00 |
| 1:00 |
| 2:00 |
| 3:00 |
| 4:00 |
| 5:00 |
| 6:00 |
| 7:00 |
| 8:00 |
| 9:00 |
| 10:00 |
| 11:00 |

Friday 6

TODAY'S GOAL

PRIORITIES
1
2
3

| 5:00 |
| 6:00 |
| 7:00 |
| 8:00 |
| 9:00 |
| 10:00 |
| 11:00 |
| 12:00 |
| 1:00 |
| 2:00 |
| 3:00 |
| 4:00 |
| 5:00 |
| 6:00 |
| 7:00 |
| 8:00 |
| 9:00 |
| 10:00 |
| 11:00 |

Saturday 7

TODAY'S GOAL

PRIORITIES
1
2
3

| 5:00 |
| 6:00 |
| 7:00 |
| 8:00 |
| 9:00 |
| 10:00 |
| 11:00 |
| 12:00 |
| 1:00 |
| 2:00 |
| 3:00 |
| 4:00 |
| 5:00 |
| 6:00 |
| 7:00 |
| 8:00 |
| 9:00 |
| 10:00 |
| 11:00 |

Sunday 8

TODAY'S GOAL

PRIORITIES
1
2
3

| 5:00 |
| 6:00 |
| 7:00 |
| 8:00 |
| 9:00 |
| 10:00 |
| 11:00 |
| 12:00 |
| 1:00 |
| 2:00 |
| 3:00 |
| 4:00 |
| 5:00 |
| 6:00 |
| 7:00 |
| 8:00 |
| 9:00 |
| 10:00 |
| 11:00 |

Gratitude box

August 9-15

This week's priority

Top priority

....
....
....

Priority

....
....
....
....

Errands

....
....
....

Events | Appointments | Due dates

....
....
....
....
....
....
....
....
....
....

"All abundance starts first in the mind."

— Anonymous

notes | ideas

Positive Habits

	M	T	W	T	F	S	S
Gratitude							
Excercise							
Meditation							
Affirmations							

July

M	T	W	T	F	S	S
			1	2	3	4
5	6	7	8	9	10	11
12	13	14	15	16	17	18
19	20	21	22	23	24	25
26	27	28	29	30	31	

August

M	T	W	T	F	S	S
						1
2	3	4	5	6	7	8
9	10	11	12	13	14	15
16	17	18	19	20	21	22
23	24	25	26	27	28	29
30	31					

Monday 9

TODAY'S GOAL

PRIORITIES
1
2
3

5:00	
6:00	
7:00	
8:00	
9:00	
10:00	
11:00	
12:00	
1:00	
2:00	
3:00	
4:00	
5:00	
6:00	
7:00	
8:00	
9:00	
10:00	
11:00	

Tuesday 10

TODAY'S GOAL

PRIORITIES
1
2
3

5:00	
6:00	
7:00	
8:00	
9:00	
10:00	
11:00	
12:00	
1:00	
2:00	
3:00	
4:00	
5:00	
6:00	
7:00	
8:00	
9:00	
10:00	
11:00	

Wednesday 11

TODAY'S GOAL

PRIORITIES
1
2
3

5:00	
6:00	
7:00	
8:00	
9:00	
10:00	
11:00	
12:00	
1:00	
2:00	
3:00	
4:00	
5:00	
6:00	
7:00	
8:00	
9:00	
10:00	
11:00	

Thursday 12

TODAY'S GOAL

PRIORITIES
1
2
3

5:00	
6:00	
7:00	
8:00	
9:00	
10:00	
11:00	
12:00	
1:00	
2:00	
3:00	
4:00	
5:00	
6:00	
7:00	
8:00	
9:00	
10:00	
11:00	

Friday 13

TODAY'S GOAL

PRIORITIES
1
2
3

5:00	
6:00	
7:00	
8:00	
9:00	
10:00	
11:00	
12:00	
1:00	
2:00	
3:00	
4:00	
5:00	
6:00	
7:00	
8:00	
9:00	
10:00	
11:00	

Saturday 14

TODAY'S GOAL

PRIORITIES
1
2
3

5:00	
6:00	
7:00	
8:00	
9:00	
10:00	
11:00	
12:00	
1:00	
2:00	
3:00	
4:00	
5:00	
6:00	
7:00	
8:00	
9:00	
10:00	
11:00	

Sunday 15

TODAY'S GOAL

PRIORITIES
1
2
3

5:00	
6:00	
7:00	
8:00	
9:00	
10:00	
11:00	
12:00	
1:00	
2:00	
3:00	
4:00	
5:00	
6:00	
7:00	
8:00	
9:00	
10:00	
11:00	

Gratitude box

August 16-22

This week's priority

Top priority

....
....
....
....

Priority

....
....
....
....

Errands

....
....
....
....

Events | Appointments | Due dates

....
....
....
....
....
....
....
....
....
....

"Most of the shadows of this life are caused by standing in one's own sunshine."

– Ralph Waldo Emerson

notes | ideas

Positive Habits

	M	T	W	T	F	S	S
Gratitude							
Excercise							
Meditation							
Affirmations							

July

M	T	W	T	F	S	S
			1	2	3	4
5	6	7	8	9	10	11
12	13	14	15	16	17	18
19	20	21	22	23	24	25
26	27	28	29	30	31	

August

M	T	W	T	F	S	S
						1
2	3	4	5	6	7	8
9	10	11	12	13	14	15
16	17	18	19	20	21	22
23	24	25	26	27	28	29
30	31					

Monday 16

PRIORITIES
1
2
3

5.00	
6.00	
7.00	
8.00	
9.00	
10.00	
11.00	
12.00	
1.00	
2.00	
3.00	
4.00	
5.00	
6.00	
7.00	
8.00	
9.00	
10.00	
11.00	

Tuesday 17

TODAY'S GOAL

PRIORITIES
1
2
3

5.00	
6.00	
7.00	
8.00	
9.00	
10.00	
11.00	
12.00	
1.00	
2.00	
3.00	
4.00	
5.00	
6.00	
7.00	
8.00	
9.00	
10.00	
11.00	

Wednesday 18

TODAY'S GOAL

PRIORITIES
1
2
3

5.00	
6.00	
7.00	
8.00	
9.00	
10.00	
11.00	
12.00	
1.00	
2.00	
3.00	
4.00	
5.00	
6.00	
7.00	
8.00	
9.00	
10.00	
11.00	

Thursday 19

TODAY'S GOAL

PRIORITIES
1
2
3

5.00	
6.00	
7.00	
8.00	
9.00	
10.00	
11.00	
12.00	
1.00	
2.00	
3.00	
4.00	
5.00	
6.00	
7.00	
8.00	
9.00	
10.00	
11.00	

Friday 20

TODAY'S GOAL

PRIORITIES
1
2
3

5.00	
6.00	
7.00	
8.00	
9.00	
10.00	
11.00	
12.00	
1.00	
2.00	
3.00	
4.00	
5.00	
6.00	
7.00	
8.00	
9.00	
10.00	
11.00	

Saturday 21

TODAY'S GOAL

PRIORITIES
1
2
3

5.00	
6.00	
7.00	
8.00	
9.00	
10.00	
11.00	
12.00	
1.00	
2.00	
3.00	
4.00	
5.00	
6.00	
7.00	
8.00	
9.00	
10.00	
11.00	

Sunday 22

TODAY'S GOAL

PRIORITIES
1
2
3

5.00	
6.00	
7.00	
8.00	
9.00	
10.00	
11.00	
12.00	
1.00	
2.00	
3.00	
4.00	
5.00	
6.00	
7.00	
8.00	
9.00	
10.00	
11.00	

Gratitude box

August 23-29

This week's priority

....
....
....
....

Priority

....
....
....
....

Errands

....
....
....

Events ǀ Appointments ǀ Due dates

....
....
....
....
....
....
....
....
....
....

"We are like magnets – like attracts like. You become and attract what you think."

– Anonymous

notes ǀ ideas

Positive Habits

	M	T	W	T	F	S	S
Gratitude							
Excercise							
Meditation							
Affirmations							

August

M	T	W	T	F	S	S
						1
2	3	4	5	6	7	8
9	10	11	12	13	14	15
16	17	18	19	20	21	22
23	24	25	26	27	28	29
30	31					

September

M	T	W	T	F	S	S
	1	2	3	4	5
6	7	8	9	10	11	12
13	14	15	16	17	18	19
20	21	22	23	24	25	26
27	28	29	30			

Monday 23

TODAY'S GOAL

PRIORITIES
1
2
3

| 5:00 |
| 6:00 |
| 7:00 |
| 8:00 |
| 9:00 |
| 10:00 |
| 11:00 |
| 12:00 |
| 1:00 |
| 2:00 |
| 3:00 |
| 4:00 |
| 5:00 |
| 6:00 |
| 7:00 |
| 8:00 |
| 9:00 |
| 10:00 |
| 11:00 |

Tuesday 24

TODAY'S GOAL

PRIORITIES
1
2
3

| 5:00 |
| 6:00 |
| 7:00 |
| 8:00 |
| 9:00 |
| 10:00 |
| 11:00 |
| 12:00 |
| 1:00 |
| 2:00 |
| 3:00 |
| 4:00 |
| 5:00 |
| 6:00 |
| 7:00 |
| 8:00 |
| 9:00 |
| 10:00 |
| 11:00 |

Wednesday 25

TODAY'S GOAL

PRIORITIES
1
2
3

| 5:00 |
| 6:00 |
| 7:00 |
| 8:00 |
| 9:00 |
| 10:00 |
| 11:00 |
| 12:00 |
| 1:00 |
| 2:00 |
| 3:00 |
| 4:00 |
| 5:00 |
| 6:00 |
| 7:00 |
| 8:00 |
| 9:00 |
| 10:00 |
| 11:00 |

Thursday 26

TODAY'S GOAL

PRIORITIES
1
2
3

| 5:00 |
| 6:00 |
| 7:00 |
| 8:00 |
| 9:00 |
| 10:00 |
| 11:00 |
| 12:00 |
| 1:00 |
| 2:00 |
| 3:00 |
| 4:00 |
| 5:00 |
| 6:00 |
| 7:00 |
| 8:00 |
| 9:00 |
| 10:00 |
| 11:00 |

Friday 27

TODAY'S GOAL

PRIORITIES
1
2
3

| 5:00 |
| 6:00 |
| 7:00 |
| 8:00 |
| 9:00 |
| 10:00 |
| 11:00 |
| 12:00 |
| 1:00 |
| 2:00 |
| 3:00 |
| 4:00 |
| 5:00 |
| 6:00 |
| 7:00 |
| 8:00 |
| 9:00 |
| 10:00 |
| 11:00 |

Saturday 28

TODAY'S GOAL

PRIORITIES
1
2
3

| 5:00 |
| 6:00 |
| 7:00 |
| 8:00 |
| 9:00 |
| 10:00 |
| 11:00 |
| 12:00 |
| 1:00 |
| 2:00 |
| 3:00 |
| 4:00 |
| 5:00 |
| 6:00 |
| 7:00 |
| 8:00 |
| 9:00 |
| 10:00 |
| 11:00 |

Sunday 29

TODAY'S GOAL

PRIORITIES
1
2
3

| 5:00 |
| 6:00 |
| 7:00 |
| 8:00 |
| 9:00 |
| 10:00 |
| 11:00 |
| 12:00 |
| 1:00 |
| 2:00 |
| 3:00 |
| 4:00 |
| 5:00 |
| 6:00 |
| 7:00 |
| 8:00 |
| 9:00 |
| 10:00 |
| 11:00 |

Gratitude box

August 30-September 5

This week's priority

Top priority

....
....
....
....

Priority

....
....
....
....

Errands

....
....
....

Events | Appointments | Due dates

....
....
....
....
....
....
....
....

"The universe likes speed. Don't delay, don't second-guess, don't doubt."

— The Secret

notes | ideas

Positive Habits

	M	T	W	T	F	S	S
Gratitude							
Excercise							
Meditation							
Affirmations							

August

M	T	W	T	F	S	S
						1
2	3	4	5	6	7	8
9	10	11	12	13	14	15
16	17	18	19	20	21	22
23	24	25	26	27	28	29
30	31					

September

M	T	W	T	F	S	S
	1	2	3	4	5
6	7	8	9	10	11	12
13	14	15	16	17	18	19
20	21	22	23	24	25	26
27	28	29	30			

Monday 30

TODAY'S GOAL

PRIORITIES
1
2
3

5:00	
6:00	
7:00	
8:00	
9:00	
10:00	
11:00	
12:00	
1:00	
2:00	
3:00	
4:00	
5:00	
6:00	
7:00	
8:00	
9:00	
10:00	
11:00	

Tuesday 31

TODAY'S GOAL

PRIORITIES
1
2
3

5:00	
6:00	
7:00	
8:00	
9:00	
10:00	
11:00	
12:00	
1:00	
2:00	
3:00	
4:00	
5:00	
6:00	
7:00	
8:00	
9:00	
10:00	
11:00	

Wednesday 1

TODAY'S GOAL

PRIORITIES
1
2
3

5:00	
6:00	
7:00	
8:00	
9:00	
10:00	
11:00	
12:00	
1:00	
2:00	
3:00	
4:00	
5:00	
6:00	
7:00	
8:00	
9:00	
10:00	
11:00	

Thursday 2

TODAY'S GOAL

PRIORITIES
1
2
3

5:00	
6:00	
7:00	
8:00	
9:00	
10:00	
11:00	
12:00	
1:00	
2:00	
3:00	
4:00	
5:00	
6:00	
7:00	
8:00	
9:00	
10:00	
11:00	

Friday 3

TODAY'S GOAL

PRIORITIES
1
2
3

5:00	
6:00	
7:00	
8:00	
9:00	
10:00	
11:00	
12:00	
1:00	
2:00	
3:00	
4:00	
5:00	
6:00	
7:00	
8:00	
9:00	
10:00	
11:00	

Saturday 4

TODAY'S GOAL

PRIORITIES
1
2
3

5:00	
6:00	
7:00	
8:00	
9:00	
10:00	
11:00	
12:00	
1:00	
2:00	
3:00	
4:00	
5:00	
6:00	
7:00	
8:00	
9:00	
10:00	
11:00	

Sunday 5

TODAY'S GOAL

PRIORITIES
1
2
3

5:00	
6:00	
7:00	
8:00	
9:00	
10:00	
11:00	
12:00	
1:00	
2:00	
3:00	
4:00	
5:00	
6:00	
7:00	
8:00	
9:00	
10:00	
11:00	

Gratitude box

Reflect on your month

When you start actively observing and understanding the invisible parts of yourself – your emotions – you'll equip yourself with the tools to make visible changes in your day-to-day life. Observe how your emotions and feelings change over weeks and months. Become aware of them and change them to more positive feelings so you can attract and manifest the life of your dreams.

Check how balanced you lived your month.

What did I learn this month?

....
....
....
....

My top 5 achievements this month

....
....
....
....

How was I feeling this month?

Optimistic
Proud
Guilty
Depressed
Peaceful
Lonely
Confused
Disapproval
Happy
Sad
Excited
Surprise
Disgust
Awful
Amazed
Fear
Anger
Disappointed
Insecure
Aggressive
Humiliated
Scared
Hurt
Mad

Did I enjoy what I was doing this month?

....
....
....
....

How did I make myself feel good?

....
....
....
....

How do I feel about my progress this month?

_____

_____

_____

_____

_____

What are the greatest insights that I have gained?

_____

_____

_____

_____

_____

What mental blocks did I encounter?

_____

_____

_____

_____

_____

What / who inspired me this month?

_____

_____

_____

_____

_____

What actions can I take to improve?

_____

_____

_____

_____

_____

2021

September

M	T	W	T	F	S	S
		1	2	3	4	5
6	7	8	9	10	11	12
13	14	15	16	17	18	19
20	21	22	23	24	25	26
27	28	29	30			

Monthly
Mood Tracker

Our Mood Tracker is a powerful and easy-to-use tool that allows you to track your emotions – or moods – on a regular basis.

You want to lead a fulfilling, happy life. All of that becomes so much simpler with the Mood Tracker. The perfect mental health support system, this Mood Tracker charts your triggers, looks at your ups and downs, and gives you permission to feel so you can understand your anxiety, support your stress relief, and become happier all around.

By tracking your moods, you may be able to determine situations or times that your mood goes up or down. Such situations are sometimes called triggers. For instance, if you notice you get depressed every time you visit your parents, that's important information that you can use to help you understand yourself better.

Reflect on emotions daily – gain insight into the patterns of your moods, triggers, coping skills, and mindsets.

Chart your emotions. Relieve your anxiety. BUILD A HAPPIER YOU!

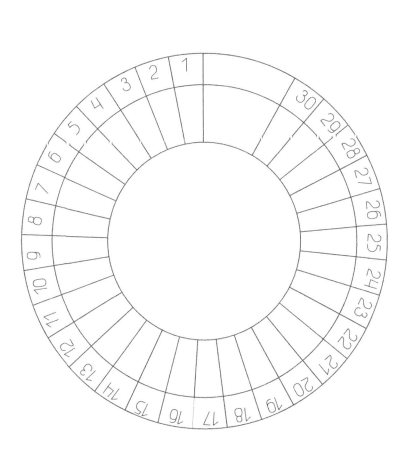

COLOR YOUR MOOD

Angry	
Annoyed	
Anxious	
Ashamed	
Confused	
Energetic	
Excited	
Exhausted	
Happy	
Sad	
Relaxed	
Productive	

Monthly Goal Planner

GOAL

REWARD

✓	ACTION STEPS	NOTES

PROGRESS TRACKER

25%   50%   75%   100%

NOTES

GOAL

REWARD

✓	ACTION STEPS	NOTES

PROGRESS TRACKER

25%   50%   75%   100%

NOTES

Monthly Habit Tracker

Monthly habit tracker can be particularly powerful on a bad day. When you're feeling down, it's easy to forget about all the progress you have already made. Habit tracking provides visual proof of your hard work — a subtle reminder of how far you've come. Plus, the empty square you see each morning can motivate you to get started because you don't want to lose your progress by breaking your streak.

COLOR   ESSENTIAL HABITS

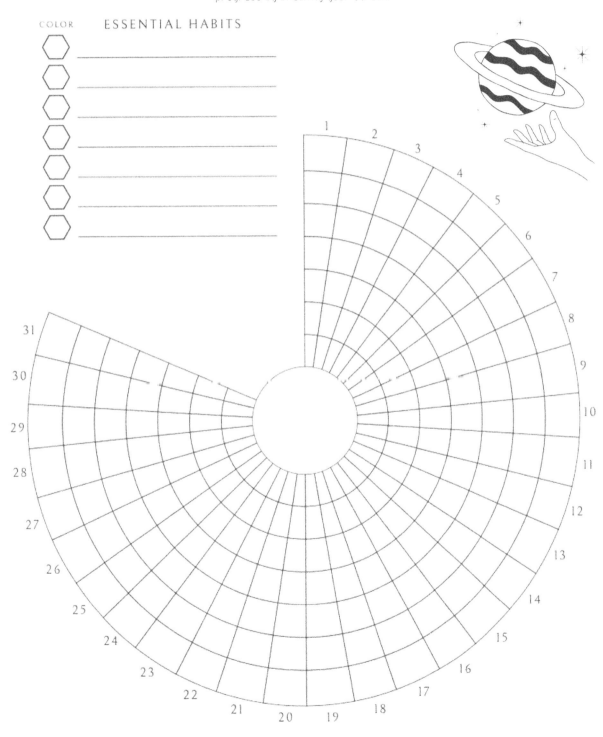

September 6-12

This week's priority

Top priority
....
....
....
....
....

Priority
....
....
....
....

Errands
....
....
....

Events | Appointments | Due dates

....
....
....
....
....
....
....
....
....
....
....

"Be thankful for what you have, you'll end up having more. If you concentrate
on what you don't have, you will never ever have enough."

– Oprah Winfrey

notes | ideas

Positive Habits

	M	T	W	T	F	S	S
Gratitude							
Excercise							
Meditation							
Affirmations							

August

M	T	W	T	F	S	S
						1
2	3	4	5	6	7	8
9	10	11	12	13	14	15
16	17	18	19	20	21	22
23	24	25	26	27	28	29
30	31					

September

M	T	W	T	F	S	S
		1	2	3	4	5
6	7	8	9	10	11	12
13	14	15	16	17	18	19
20	21	22	23	24	25	26
27	28	29	30			

Monday 6
Labor Day

TODAY'S GOAL

PRIORITIES
1
2
3

Time	
5:00	
6:00	
7:00	
8:00	
9:00	
10:00	
11:00	
12:00	
1:00	
2:00	
3:00	
4:00	
5:00	
6:00	
7:00	
8:00	
9:00	
10:00	
11:00	

Tuesday 7

TODAY'S GOAL

PRIORITIES
1
2
3

Time	
5:00	
6:00	
7:00	
8:00	
9:00	
10:00	
11:00	
12:00	
1:00	
2:00	
3:00	
4:00	
5:00	
6:00	
7:00	
8:00	
9:00	
10:00	
11:00	

Wednesday 8

TODAY'S GOAL

PRIORITIES
1
2
3

Time	
5:00	
6:00	
7:00	
8:00	
9:00	
10:00	
11:00	
12:00	
1:00	
2:00	
3:00	
4:00	
5:00	
6:00	
7:00	
8:00	
9:00	
10:00	
11:00	

Thursday 9

TODAY'S GOAL

PRIORITIES
1
2
3

Time	
5:00	
6:00	
7:00	
8:00	
9:00	
10:00	
11:00	
12:00	
1:00	
2:00	
3:00	
4:00	
5:00	
6:00	
7:00	
8:00	
9:00	
10:00	
11:00	

Friday 10

TODAY'S GOAL

PRIORITIES
1
2
3

Time	
5:00	
6:00	
7:00	
8:00	
9:00	
10:00	
11:00	
12:00	
1:00	
2:00	
3:00	
4:00	
5:00	
6:00	
7:00	
8:00	
9:00	
10:00	
11:00	

Saturday 11

TODAY'S GOAL

PRIORITIES
1
2
3

Time	
5:00	
6:00	
7:00	
8:00	
9:00	
10:00	
11:00	
12:00	
1:00	
2:00	
3:00	
4:00	
5:00	
6:00	
7:00	
8:00	
9:00	
10:00	
11:00	

Sunday 12

TODAY'S GOAL

PRIORITIES
1
2
3

Time	
5:00	
6:00	
7:00	
8:00	
9:00	
10:00	
11:00	
12:00	
1:00	
2:00	
3:00	
4:00	
5:00	
6:00	
7:00	
8:00	
9:00	
10:00	
11:00	

Gratitude box

September 13-19

This week's priority

Top priority

....
....
....
....
....

Priority

....
....
....
....

Errands

....
....
....

Events | Appointments | Due dates

....
....
....
....
....
....
....
....
....
....
....
....

"Richness is not about what you have. It is about who you are."

— Bob Proctor

notes | ideas

Positive Habits

	M	T	W	T	F	S	S
Gratitude							
Excercise							
Meditation							
Affirmations							

August

M	T	W	T	F	S	S
						1
2	3	4	5	6	7	8
9	10	11	12	13	14	15
16	17	18	19	20	21	22
23	24	25	26	27	28	29
30	31					

September

M	T	W	T	F	S	S
		1	2	3	4	5
6	7	8	9	10	11	12
13	14	15	16	17	18	19
20	21	22	23	24	25	26
27	28	29	30			

Monday 13

TODAY'S GOAL

PRIORITIES

1
2
3

5:00	
6:00	
7:00	
8:00	
9:00	
10:00	
11:00	
12:00	
1:00	
2:00	
3:00	
4:00	
5:00	
6:00	
7:00	
8:00	
9:00	
10:00	
11:00	

Tuesday 14

TODAY'S GOAL

PRIORITIES

1
2
3

5:00	
6:00	
7:00	
8:00	
9:00	
10:00	
11:00	
12:00	
1:00	
2:00	
3:00	
4:00	
5:00	
6:00	
7:00	
8:00	
9:00	
10:00	
11:00	

Wednesday 15

TODAY'S GOAL

PRIORITIES

1
2
3

5:00	
6:00	
7:00	
8:00	
9:00	
10:00	
11:00	
12:00	
1:00	
2:00	
3:00	
4:00	
5:00	
6:00	
7:00	
8:00	
9:00	
10:00	
11:00	

Thursday 16

TODAY'S GOAL

PRIORITIES

1
2
3

5:00	
6:00	
7:00	
8:00	
9:00	
10:00	
11:00	
12:00	
1:00	
2:00	
3:00	
4:00	
5:00	
6:00	
7:00	
8:00	
9:00	
10:00	
11:00	

Friday 17

TODAY'S GOAL

PRIORITIES

1
2
3

5:00	
6:00	
7:00	
8:00	
9:00	
10:00	
11:00	
12:00	
1:00	
2:00	
3:00	
4:00	
5:00	
6:00	
7:00	
8:00	
9:00	
10:00	
11:00	

Saturday 18

TODAY'S GOAL

PRIORITIES

1
2
3

5:00	
6:00	
7:00	
8:00	
9:00	
10:00	
11:00	
12:00	
1:00	
2:00	
3:00	
4:00	
5:00	
6:00	
7:00	
8:00	
9:00	
10:00	
11:00	

Sunday 19

TODAY'S GOAL

PRIORITIES

1
2
3

5:00	
6:00	
7:00	
8:00	
9:00	
10:00	
11:00	
12:00	
1:00	
2:00	
3:00	
4:00	
5:00	
6:00	
7:00	
8:00	
9:00	
10:00	
11:00	

Gratitude box

September 20-26

This week's priority

Top priority

....
....
....
....

Priority

....
....
....
....

Errands

....
....
....

Events | Appointments | Due dates

....
....
....
....
....
....
....
....

"We do not need magic to transform our world. We carry all of the power we need inside ourselves already."

— J. K. Rowling

notes | ideas

Positive Habits

	M	T	W	T	F	S	S
Gratitude							
Excercise							
Meditation							
Affirmations							

September

M	T	W	T	F	S	S
		1	2	3	4	5
6	7	8	9	10	11	12
13	14	15	16	17	18	19
20	21	22	23	24	25	26
27	28	29	30			

October

M	T	W	T	F	S	S
				1	2	3
4	5	6	7	8	9	10
11	12	13	14	15	16	17
18	19	20	21	22	23	24
25	26	27	28	29	30	31

Monday 20

TODAY'S GOAL

PRIORITIES
1
2
3

| 5:00 |
| 6:00 |
| 7:00 |
| 8:00 |
| 9:00 |
| 10:00 |
| 11:00 |
| 12:00 |
| 1:00 |
| 2:00 |
| 3:00 |
| 4:00 |
| 5:00 |
| 6:00 |
| 7:00 |
| 8:00 |
| 9:00 |
| 10:00 |
| 11:00 |

Tuesday 21

TODAY'S GOAL

PRIORITIES
1
2
3

| 5:00 |
| 6:00 |
| 7:00 |
| 8:00 |
| 9:00 |
| 10:00 |
| 11:00 |
| 12:00 |
| 1:00 |
| 2:00 |
| 3:00 |
| 4:00 |
| 5:00 |
| 6:00 |
| 7:00 |
| 8:00 |
| 9:00 |
| 10:00 |
| 11:00 |

Wednesday 22

TODAY'S GOAL

PRIORITIES
1
2
3

| 5:00 |
| 6:00 |
| 7:00 |
| 8:00 |
| 9:00 |
| 10:00 |
| 11:00 |
| 12:00 |
| 1:00 |
| 2:00 |
| 3:00 |
| 4:00 |
| 5:00 |
| 6:00 |
| 7:00 |
| 8:00 |
| 9:00 |
| 10:00 |
| 11:00 |

Thursday 23

TODAY'S GOAL

PRIORITIES
1
2
3

| 5:00 |
| 6:00 |
| 7:00 |
| 8:00 |
| 9:00 |
| 10:00 |
| 11:00 |
| 12:00 |
| 1:00 |
| 2:00 |
| 3:00 |
| 4:00 |
| 5:00 |
| 6:00 |
| 7:00 |
| 8:00 |
| 9:00 |
| 10:00 |
| 11:00 |

Friday 24

TODAY'S GOAL

PRIORITIES
1
2
3

| 5:00 |
| 6:00 |
| 7:00 |
| 8:00 |
| 9:00 |
| 10:00 |
| 11:00 |
| 12:00 |
| 1:00 |
| 2:00 |
| 3:00 |
| 4:00 |
| 5:00 |
| 6:00 |
| 7:00 |
| 8:00 |
| 9:00 |
| 10:00 |
| 11:00 |

Saturday 25

TODAY'S GOAL

PRIORITIES
1
2
3

| 5:00 |
| 6:00 |
| 7:00 |
| 8:00 |
| 9:00 |
| 10:00 |
| 11:00 |
| 12:00 |
| 1:00 |
| 2:00 |
| 3:00 |
| 4:00 |
| 5:00 |
| 6:00 |
| 7:00 |
| 8:00 |
| 9:00 |
| 10:00 |
| 11:00 |

Sunday 26

TODAY'S GOAL

PRIORITIES
1
2
3

| 5:00 |
| 6:00 |
| 7:00 |
| 8:00 |
| 9:00 |
| 10:00 |
| 11:00 |
| 12:00 |
| 1:00 |
| 2:00 |
| 3:00 |
| 4:00 |
| 5:00 |
| 6:00 |
| 7:00 |
| 8:00 |
| 9:00 |
| 10:00 |
| 11:00 |

Gratitude box

September 27–October 3

This week's priority

Top priority

....
....
....
....

Priority

....
....
....
....

Errands

....
....

Events | Appointments | Due dates

....
....
....
....
....
....
....
....
....
....

"Once you replace negative thoughts with positive ones, you'll start having positive results."

– Willie Nelson

notes | ideas

Positive Habits

	M	T	W	T	F	S	S
Gratitude							
Excercise							
Meditation							
Affirmations							

September

M	T	W	T	F	S	S
		1	2	3	4	5
6	7	8	9	10	11	12
13	14	15	16	17	18	19
20	21	22	23	24	25	26
27	28	29	30			

October

M	T	W	T	F	S	S
				1	2	3
4	5	6	7	8	9	10
11	12	13	14	15	16	17
18	19	20	21	22	23	24
25	26	27	28	29	30	31

Monday 27

TODAY'S GOAL

PRIORITIES
1
2
3

5:00	
6:00	
7:00	
8:00	
9:00	
10:00	
11:00	
12:00	
1:00	
2:00	
3:00	
4:00	
5:00	
6:00	
7:00	
8:00	
9:00	
10:00	
11:00	

Tuesday 28

TODAY'S GOAL

PRIORITIES
1
2
3

5:00	
6:00	
7:00	
8:00	
9:00	
10:00	
11:00	
12:00	
1:00	
2:00	
3:00	
4:00	
5:00	
6:00	
7:00	
8:00	
9:00	
10:00	
11:00	

Wednesday 29

TODAY'S GOAL

PRIORITIES
1
2
3

5:00	
6:00	
7:00	
8:00	
9:00	
10:00	
11:00	
12:00	
1:00	
2:00	
3:00	
4:00	
5:00	
6:00	
7:00	
8:00	
9:00	
10:00	
11:00	

Thursday 30

TODAY'S GOAL

PRIORITIES
1
2
3

5:00	
6:00	
7:00	
8:00	
9:00	
10:00	
11:00	
12:00	
1:00	
2:00	
3:00	
4:00	
5:00	
6:00	
7:00	
8:00	
9:00	
10:00	
11:00	

Friday 1

TODAY'S GOAL

PRIORITIES
1
2
3

5:00	
6:00	
7:00	
8:00	
9:00	
10:00	
11:00	
12:00	
1:00	
2:00	
3:00	
4:00	
5:00	
6:00	
7:00	
8:00	
9:00	
10:00	
11:00	

Saturday 2

TODAY'S GOAL

PRIORITIES
1
2
3

5:00	
6:00	
7:00	
8:00	
9:00	
10:00	
11:00	
12:00	
1:00	
2:00	
3:00	
4:00	
5:00	
6:00	
7:00	
8:00	
9:00	
10:00	
11:00	

Sunday 3

TODAY'S GOAL

PRIORITIES
1
2
3

5:00	
6:00	
7:00	
8:00	
9:00	
10:00	
11:00	
12:00	
1:00	
2:00	
3:00	
4:00	
5:00	
6:00	
7:00	
8:00	
9:00	
10:00	
11:00	

Gratitude box

Reflect on your month

When you start actively observing and understanding the invisible parts of yourself – your emotions – you'll equip yourself with the tools to make visible changes in your day-to-day life. Observe how your emotions and feelings change over weeks and months. Become aware of them and change them to more positive feelings so you can attract and manifest the life of your dreams.

Check how balanced you lived your month.

What did I learn this month?

....

....

....

....

My top 5 achievements this month

....

....

....

....

How was I feeling this month?

Optimistic · Proud · Guilty · Depressed · Peaceful · Lonely · Confused · Disapproval · Happy · Sad · Excited · Surprise · Disgust · Awful · Amazed · Anger · Disappointed · Insecure · Fear · Aggressive · Humiliated · Scared · Hurt · Mad

Did I enjoy what I was doing this month?

....

....

....

....

....

How did I make myself feel good?

....

....

....

....

....

How do I feel about my progress this month?

What are the greatest insights that I have gained?

What mental blocks did I encounter?

What / who inspired me this month?

What actions can I take to improve?

2021

October

M	T	W	T	F	S	S
				1	2	3
4	5	6	7	8	9	10
11	12	13	14	15	16	17
18	19	20	21	22	23	24
25	26	27	28	29	30	31

Monthly
Mood Tracker

Our Mood Tracker is a powerful and easy-to-use tool that allows you to track your emotions – or moods – on a regular basis.

You want to lead a fulfilling, happy life. All of that becomes so much simpler with the Mood Tracker. The perfect mental health support system, this Mood Tracker charts your triggers, looks at your ups and downs, and gives you permission to feel so you can understand your anxiety, support your stress relief, and become happier all around.

By tracking your moods, you may be able to determine situations or times that your mood goes up or down. Such situations are sometimes called triggers. For instance, if you notice you get depressed every time you visit your parents, that's important information that you can use to help you understand yourself better.

Reflect on emotions daily – gain insight into the patterns of your moods, triggers, coping skills, and mindsets.

Chart your emotions. Relieve your anxiety. BUILD A HAPPIER YOU!

COLOR YOUR MOOD

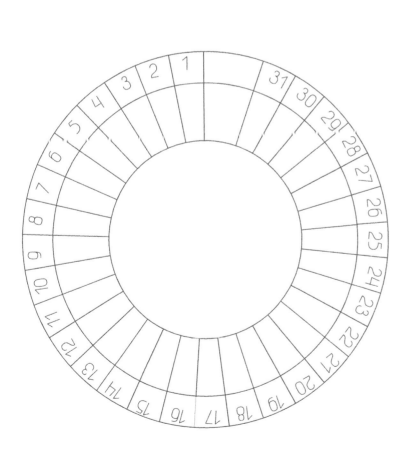

Angry	
Annoyed	
Anxious	
Ashamed	
Confused	
Energetic	
Excited	
Exhausted	
Happy	
Sad	
Relaxed	
Productive	

Monthly Goal Planner

GOAL

REWARD

⌄	ACTION STEPS	NOTES

PROGRESS TRACKER

    25%   50%   75%   100%

NOTES

GOAL

REWARD

⌄	ACTION STEPS	NOTES

PROGRESS TRACKER

    25%   50%   75%   100%

NOTES

Monthly Habit Tracker

Monthly habit tracker can be particularly powerful on a bad day. When you're feeling down, it's easy to forget about all the progress you have already made. Habit tracking provides visual proof of your hard work – a subtle reminder of how far you've come. Plus, the empty square you see each morning can motivate you to get started because you don't want to lose your progress by breaking your streak.

COLOR   ESSENTIAL HABITS

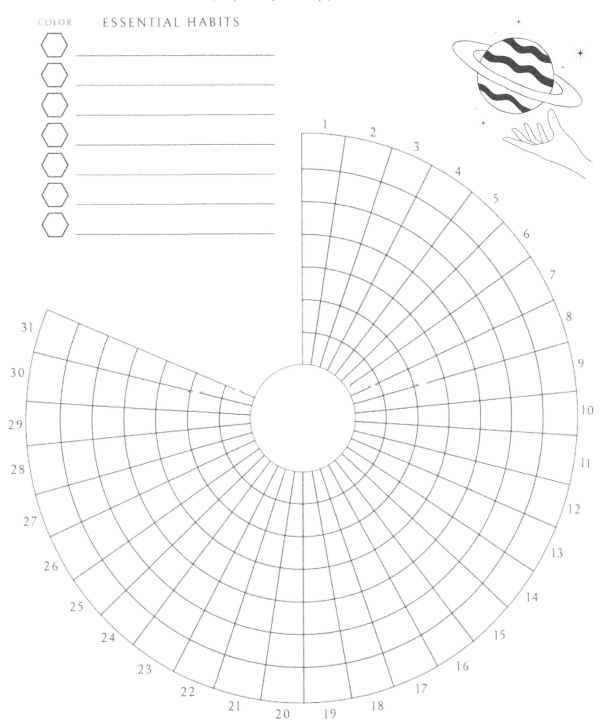

October 4-10

This week's priority

Top priority

....
....
....
....

Priority

....
....
....
....

Errands

....
....
....

Events | Appointments | Due dates

....
....
....
....
....
....
....
....
....
....
....

"See yourself living in abundance and you will attract it."

– Rhonda Byrne

notes | ideas

Positive Habits

	M	T	W	T	F	S	S
Gratitude							
Excercise							
Meditation							
Affirmations							

September

M	T	W	T	F	S	S
		1	2	3	4	5
6	7	8	9	10	11	12
13	14	15	16	17	18	19
20	21	22	23	24	25	26
27	28	29	30			

October

M	T	W	T	F	S	S
			1	2	3
4	5	6	7	8	9	10
11	12	13	14	15	16	17
18	19	20	21	22	23	24
25	26	27	28	29	30	31

Monday 4

TODAY'S GOAL

PRIORITIES
1
2
3

5:00	
6:00	
7:00	
8:00	
9:00	
10:00	
11:00	
12:00	
1:00	
2:00	
3:00	
4:00	
5:00	
6:00	
7:00	
8:00	
9:00	
10:00	
11:00	

Tuesday 5

TODAY'S GOAL

PRIORITIES
1
2
3

5:00	
6:00	
7:00	
8:00	
9:00	
10:00	
11:00	
12:00	
1:00	
2:00	
3:00	
4:00	
5:00	
6:00	
7:00	
8:00	
9:00	
10:00	
11:00	

Wednesday 6

TODAY'S GOAL

PRIORITIES
1
2
3

5:00	
6:00	
7:00	
8:00	
9:00	
10:00	
11:00	
12:00	
1:00	
2:00	
3:00	
4:00	
5:00	
6:00	
7:00	
8:00	
9:00	
10:00	
11:00	

Thursday 7

TODAY'S GOAL

PRIORITIES
1
2
3

5:00	
6:00	
7:00	
8:00	
9:00	
10:00	
11:00	
12:00	
1:00	
2:00	
3:00	
4:00	
5:00	
6:00	
7:00	
8:00	
9:00	
10:00	
11:00	

Friday 8

TODAY'S GOAL

PRIORITIES
1
2
3

5:00	
6:00	
7:00	
8:00	
9:00	
10:00	
11:00	
12:00	
1:00	
2:00	
3:00	
4:00	
5:00	
6:00	
7:00	
8:00	
9:00	
10:00	
11:00	

Saturday 9

TODAY'S GOAL

PRIORITIES
1
2
3

5:00	
6:00	
7:00	
8:00	
9:00	
10:00	
11:00	
12:00	
1:00	
2:00	
3:00	
4:00	
5:00	
6:00	
7:00	
8:00	
9:00	
10:00	
11:00	

Sunday 10

TODAY'S GOAL

PRIORITIES
1
2
3

5:00	
6:00	
7:00	
8:00	
9:00	
10:00	
11:00	
12:00	
1:00	
2:00	
3:00	
4:00	
5:00	
6:00	
7:00	
8:00	
9:00	
10:00	
11:00	

Gratitude box

October 11-17

This week's priority

Top priority

....
....
....
....

Priority

....
....
....
....

Errands

....
....
....

Events | Appointments | Due dates

....
....
....
....
....
....
....
....
....
....

"Look forward to where you want to be and spend no time complaining about where you are."

– Esther Hicks

notes | ideas

Positive Habits

	M	T	W	T	F	S	S
Gratitude							
Excercise							
Meditation							
Affirmations							

September

M	T	W	T	F	S	S
		1	2	3	4	5
6	7	8	9	10	11	12
13	14	15	16	17	18	19
20	21	22	23	24	25	26
27	28	29	30			

October

M	T	W	T	F	S	S
			1	2	3
4	5	6	7	8	9	10
11	12	13	14	15	16	17
18	19	20	21	22	23	24
25	26	27	28	29	30	31

Monday 11
Columbus Day

TODAY'S GOAL

PRIORITIES
1
2
3

5:00	
6:00	
7:00	
8:00	
9:00	
10:00	
11:00	
12:00	
1:00	
2:00	
3:00	
4:00	
5:00	
6:00	
7:00	
8:00	
9:00	
10:00	
11:00	

Tuesday 12

TODAY'S GOAL

PRIORITIES
1
2
3

5:00	
6:00	
7:00	
8:00	
9:00	
10:00	
11:00	
12:00	
1:00	
2:00	
3:00	
4:00	
5:00	
6:00	
7:00	
8:00	
9:00	
10:00	
11:00	

Wednesday 13

TODAY'S GOAL

PRIORITIES
1
2
3

5:00	
6:00	
7:00	
8:00	
9:00	
10:00	
11:00	
12:00	
1:00	
2:00	
3:00	
4:00	
5:00	
6:00	
7:00	
8:00	
9:00	
10:00	
11:00	

Thursday 14

TODAY'S GOAL

PRIORITIES
1
2
3

5:00	
6:00	
7:00	
8:00	
9:00	
10:00	
11:00	
12:00	
1:00	
2:00	
3:00	
4:00	
5:00	
6:00	
7:00	
8:00	
9:00	
10:00	
11:00	

Friday 15

TODAY'S GOAL

PRIORITIES
1
2
3

5:00	
6:00	
7:00	
8:00	
9:00	
10:00	
11:00	
12:00	
1:00	
2:00	
3:00	
4:00	
5:00	
6:00	
7:00	
8:00	
9:00	
10:00	
11:00	

Saturday 16

TODAY'S GOAL

PRIORITIES
1
2
3

5:00	
6:00	
7:00	
8:00	
9:00	
10:00	
11:00	
12:00	
1:00	
2:00	
3:00	
4:00	
5:00	
6:00	
7:00	
8:00	
9:00	
10:00	
11:00	

Sunday 17

TODAY'S GOAL

PRIORITIES
1
2
3

5:00	
6:00	
7:00	
8:00	
9:00	
10:00	
11:00	
12:00	
1:00	
2:00	
3:00	
4:00	
5:00	
6:00	
7:00	
8:00	
9:00	
10:00	
11:00	

Gratitude box

October 18-24

This week's priority

Top priority

....
....
....
....

Priority

....
....
....
....

Errands

....
....
....

Events | Appointments | Due dates

....
....
....
....
....
....
....
....
....
....

"To achieve goals you've never achieved before, you need to start doing things you've never done before."

– Stephen Covey

notes | ideas

Positive Habits

	M	T	W	T	F	S	S
Gratitude							
Excercise							
Meditation							
Affirmations							

October

M	T	W	T	F	S	S
				1	2	3
4	5	6	7	8	9	10
11	12	13	14	15	16	17
18	19	20	21	22	23	24
25	26	27	28	29	30	31

November

M	T	W	T	F	S	S
1	2	3	4	5	6	7
8	9	10	11	12	13	14
15	16	17	18	19	20	21
22	23	24	25	26	27	28
29	30					

Monday 18	Tuesday 19	Wednesday 20	Thursday 21
TODAY'S GOAL	TODAY'S GOAL	TODAY'S GOAL	TODAY'S GOAL
PRIORITIES	PRIORITIES	PRIORITIES	PRIORITIES
1	1	1	1
2	2	2	2
3	3	3	3
5.00	5.00	5.00	5.00
6.00	6.00	6.00	6.00
7.00	7.00	7.00	7.00
8.00	8.00	8.00	8.00
9.00	9.00	9.00	9.00
10.00	10.00	10.00	10.00
11.00	11.00	11.00	11.00
12.00	12.00	12.00	12.00
1.00	1.00	1.00	1.00
2.00	2.00	2.00	2.00
3.00	3.00	3.00	3.00
4.00	4.00	4.00	4.00
5.00	5.00	5.00	5.00
6.00	6.00	6.00	6.00
7.00	7.00	7.00	7.00
8.00	8.00	8.00	8.00
9.00	9.00	9.00	9.00
10.00	10.00	10.00	10.00
11.00	11.00	11.00	11.00

Friday 22	Saturday 23	Sunday 24	Gratitude box
TODAY'S GOAL	TODAY'S GOAL	TODAY'S GOAL	
PRIORITIES	PRIORITIES	PRIORITIES	
1	1	1	
2	2	2	
3	3	3	
5.00	5.00	5.00	
6.00	6.00	6.00	
7.00	7.00	7.00	
8.00	8.00	8.00	
9.00	9.00	9.00	
10.00	10.00	10.00	
11.00	11.00	11.00	
12.00	12.00	12.00	
1.00	1.00	1.00	
2.00	2.00	2.00	
3.00	3.00	3.00	
4.00	4.00	4.00	
5.00	5.00	5.00	
6.00	6.00	6.00	
7.00	7.00	7.00	
8.00	8.00	8.00	
9.00	9.00	9.00	
10.00	10.00	10.00	
11.00	11.00	11.00	

October 25-31

This week's priority

Top priority

....
....
....
....
....

Priority

....
....
....
....

Errands

....
....

notes | ideas

Events | Appointments | Due dates

....
....
....
....
....
....
....
....
....
....

"You can begin to shape your own destiny by the attitude that you keep."

– Michael Beckwith

Positive Habits

	M	T	W	T	F	S	S
Gratitude							
Excercise							
Meditation							
Affirmations							

October

M	T	W	T	F	S	S
				1	2	3
4	5	6	7	8	9	10
11	12	13	14	15	16	17
18	19	20	21	22	23	24
25	26	27	28	29	30	31

November

M	T	W	T	F	S	S
1	2	3	4	5	6	7
8	9	10	11	12	13	14
15	16	17	18	19	20	21
22	23	24	25	26	27	28
29	30					

Monday 25

TODAY'S GOAL

PRIORITIES
1
2
3

5:00	
6:00	
7:00	
8:00	
9:00	
10:00	
11:00	
12:00	
1:00	
2:00	
3:00	
4:00	
5:00	
6:00	
7:00	
8:00	
9:00	
10:00	
11:00	

Tuesday 26

TODAY'S GOAL

PRIORITIES
1
2
3

5:00	
6:00	
7:00	
8:00	
9:00	
10:00	
11:00	
12:00	
1:00	
2:00	
3:00	
4:00	
5:00	
6:00	
7:00	
8:00	
9:00	
10:00	
11:00	

Wednesday 27

TODAY'S GOAL

PRIORITIES
1
2
3

5:00	
6:00	
7:00	
8:00	
9:00	
10:00	
11:00	
12:00	
1:00	
2:00	
3:00	
4:00	
5:00	
6:00	
7:00	
8:00	
9:00	
10:00	
11:00	

Thursday 28

TODAY'S GOAL

PRIORITIES
1
2
3

5:00	
6:00	
7:00	
8:00	
9:00	
10:00	
11:00	
12:00	
1:00	
2:00	
3:00	
4:00	
5:00	
6:00	
7:00	
8:00	
9:00	
10:00	
11:00	

Friday 29

TODAY'S GOAL

PRIORITIES
1
2
3

5:00	
6:00	
7:00	
8:00	
9:00	
10:00	
11:00	
12:00	
1:00	
2:00	
3:00	
4:00	
5:00	
6:00	
7:00	
8:00	
9:00	
10:00	
11:00	

Saturday 30

TODAY'S GOAL

PRIORITIES
1
2
3

5:00	
6:00	
7:00	
8:00	
9:00	
10:00	
11:00	
12:00	
1:00	
2:00	
3:00	
4:00	
5:00	
6:00	
7:00	
8:00	
9:00	
10:00	
11:00	

Sunday 31

Halloween

TODAY'S GOAL

PRIORITIES
1
2
3

5:00	
6:00	
7:00	
8:00	
9:00	
10:00	
11:00	
12:00	
1:00	
2:00	
3:00	
4:00	
5:00	
6:00	
7:00	
8:00	
9:00	
10:00	
11:00	

Gratitude box

Reflect on your month

When you start actively observing and understanding the invisible parts of yourself – your emotions – you'll equip yourself with the tools to make visible changes in your day-to-day life. Observe how your emotions and feelings change over weeks and months. Become aware of them and change them to more positive feelings so you can attract and manifest the life of your dreams.

Check how balanced you lived your month.

What did I learn this month?

....

....

....

....

My top 5 achievements this month

....

....

....

....

How was I feeling this month?

Did I enjoy what I was doing this month?

....

....

....

....

How did I make myself feel good?

....

....

....

....

How do I feel about my progress this month?

_____
_____
_____
_____
_____

What are the greatest insights that I have gained?

_____
_____
_____
_____
_____

What mental blocks did I encounter?

_____
_____
_____
_____
_____

What / who inspired me this month?

_____
_____
_____
_____
_____

What actions can I take to improve?

_____
_____
_____
_____
_____

2021

November

M	T	W	T	F	S	S
1	2	3	4	5	6	7
8	9	10	11	12	13	14
15	16	17	18	19	20	21
22	23	24	25	26	27	28
29	30					

Monthly
Mood Tracker

Our Mood Tracker is a powerful and easy-to-use tool that allows you to track your emotions – or moods – on a regular basis.

You want to lead a fulfilling, happy life. All of that becomes so much simpler with the Mood Tracker. The perfect mental health support system, this Mood Tracker charts your triggers, looks at your ups and downs, and gives you permission to feel so you can understand your anxiety, support your stress relief, and become happier all around.

By tracking your moods, you may be able to determine situations or times that your mood goes up or down. Such situations are sometimes called triggers. For instance, if you notice you get depressed every time you visit your parents, that's important information that you can use to help you understand yourself better.

Reflect on emotions daily – gain insight into the patterns of your moods, triggers, coping skills, and mindsets.

Chart your emotions. Relieve your anxiety. BUILD A HAPPIER YOU!

COLOR YOUR MOOD

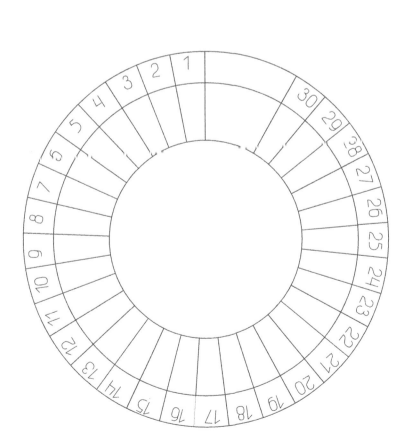

Angry	
Annoyed	
Anxious	
Ashamed	
Confused	
Energetic	
Excited	
Exhausted	
Happy	
Sad	
Relaxed	
Productive	

Monthly Goal Planner

GOAL

REWARD

⌄	ACTION STEPS	NOTES

PROGRESS TRACKER

25%   50%   75%   100%

NOTES

GOAL

REWARD

⌄	ACTION STEPS	NOTES

PROGRESS TRACKER

25%   50%   75%   100%

NOTES

Monthly
Mood Tracker

Our Mood Tracker is a powerful and easy-to-use tool that allows you to track your emotions – or moods – on a regular basis.

You want to lead a fulfilling, happy life. All of that becomes so much simpler with the Mood Tracker. The perfect mental health support system, this Mood Tracker charts your triggers, looks at your ups and downs, and gives you permission to feel so you can understand your anxiety, support your stress relief, and become happier all around.

By tracking your moods, you may be able to determine situations or times that your mood goes up or down. Such situations are sometimes called triggers. For instance, if you notice you get depressed every time you visit your parents, that's important information that you can use to help you understand yourself better.

Reflect on emotions daily – gain insight into the patterns of your moods, triggers, coping skills, and mindsets.

Chart your emotions. Relieve your anxiety. BUILD A HAPPIER YOU!

COLOR YOUR MOOD

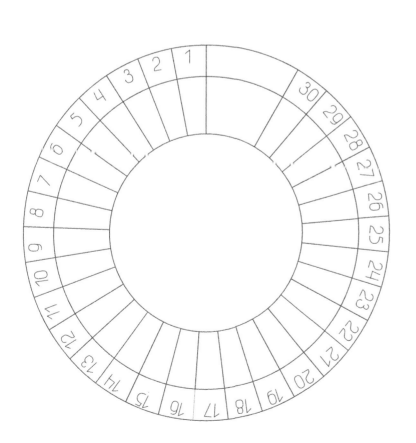

Angry	
Annoyed	
Anxious	
Ashamed	
Confused	
Energetic	
Excited	
Exhausted	
Happy	
Sad	
Relaxed	
Productive	

Monthly Goal Planner

GOAL

REWARD

✓	ACTION STEPS	NOTES

PROGRESS TRACKER

25%　　　　　50%　　　　　75%　　　　　100%

NOTES

GOAL

REWARD

✓	ACTION STEPS	NOTES

PROGRESS TRACKER

25%　　　　　50%　　　　　75%　　　　　100%

NOTES

Monthly Habit Tracker

Monthly habit tracker can be particularly powerful on a bad day. When you're feeling down, it's easy to forget about all the progress you have already made. Habit tracking provides visual proof of your hard work – a subtle reminder of how far you've come. Plus, the empty square you see each morning can motivate you to get started because you don't want to lose your progress by breaking your streak.

COLOR   ESSENTIAL HABITS

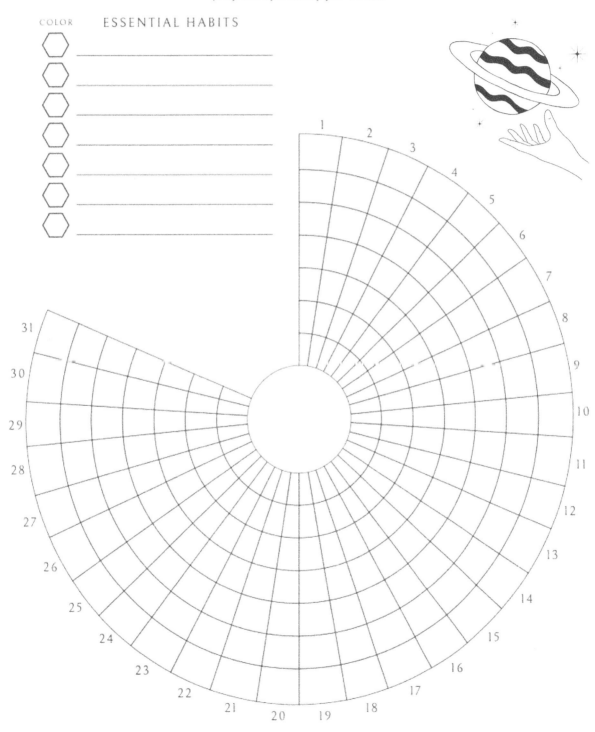

November 1-7

This week's priority

Top priority

....
....
....
....

Priority

....
....
....
....

Errands

....
....

Events | Appointments | Due dates

....
....
....
....
....
....
....
....
....
....
....

"Have faith in the magic and miracles of life, for only
those that do get to experience them."

– Hal Elrod

notes | ideas

Positive Habits

	M	T	W	T	F	S	S
Gratitude							
Excercise							
Meditation							
Affirmations							

October

M	T	W	T	F	S	S
				1	2	3
4	5	6	7	8	9	10
11	12	13	14	15	16	17
18	19	20	21	22	23	24
25	26	27	28	29	30	31

November

M	T	W	T	F	S	S
1	2	3	4	5	6	7
8	9	10	11	12	13	14
15	16	17	18	19	20	21
22	23	24	25	26	27	28
29	30					

Monday 1

TODAY'S GOAL

PRIORITIES
1
2
3

5:00	
6:00	
7:00	
8:00	
9:00	
10:00	
11:00	
12:00	
1:00	
2:00	
3:00	
4:00	
5:00	
6:00	
7:00	
8:00	
9:00	
10:00	
11:00	

Tuesday 2

TODAY'S GOAL

PRIORITIES
1
2
3

5:00	
6:00	
7:00	
8:00	
9:00	
10:00	
11:00	
12:00	
1:00	
2:00	
3:00	
4:00	
5:00	
6:00	
7:00	
8:00	
9:00	
10:00	
11:00	

Wednesday 3

TODAY'S GOAL

PRIORITIES
1
2
3

5:00	
6:00	
7:00	
8:00	
9:00	
10:00	
11:00	
12:00	
1:00	
2:00	
3:00	
4:00	
5:00	
6:00	
7:00	
8:00	
9:00	
10:00	
11:00	

Thursday 4

TODAY'S GOAL

PRIORITIES
1
2
3

5:00	
6:00	
7:00	
8:00	
9:00	
10:00	
11:00	
12:00	
1:00	
2:00	
3:00	
4:00	
5:00	
6:00	
7:00	
8:00	
9:00	
10:00	
11:00	

Friday 5

TODAY'S GOAL

PRIORITIES
1
2
3

5:00	
6:00	
7:00	
8:00	
9:00	
10:00	
11:00	
12:00	
1:00	
2:00	
3:00	
4:00	
5:00	
6:00	
7:00	
8:00	
9:00	
10:00	
11:00	

Saturday 6

TODAY'S GOAL

PRIORITIES
1
2
3

5:00	
6:00	
7:00	
8:00	
9:00	
10:00	
11:00	
12:00	
1:00	
2:00	
3:00	
4:00	
5:00	
6:00	
7:00	
8:00	
9:00	
10:00	
11:00	

Sunday 7

TODAY'S GOAL

PRIORITIES
1
2
3

5:00	
6:00	
7:00	
8:00	
9:00	
10:00	
11:00	
12:00	
1:00	
2:00	
3:00	
4:00	
5:00	
6:00	
7:00	
8:00	
9:00	
10:00	
11:00	

Gratitude box

November 8-14

This week's priority

Top priority

....
....
....
....

Priority

....
....
....
....

Errands

....
....
....

Events | Appointments | Due dates

....
....
....
....
....
....
....
....
....
....
....
....

"If you want to be happy, make someone else happy. If you want to find the right person in your life, be the right person. If you want to see change in the world, become the change you want to see."

– Deepak Chopra

notes | ideas

Positive Habits

	M	T	W	T	F	S	S
Gratitude							
Excercise							
Meditation							
Affirmations							

October

M	T	W	T	F	S	S
				1	2	3
4	5	6	7	8	9	10
11	12	13	14	15	16	17
18	19	20	21	22	23	24
25	26	27	28	29	30	31

November

M	T	W	T	F	S	S
1	2	3	4	5	6	7
8	9	10	11	12	13	14
15	16	17	18	19	20	21
22	23	24	25	26	27	28
29	30					

Monday 8

TODAY'S GOAL

PRIORITIES

1
2
3

5:00
6:00
7:00
8:00
9:00
10:00
11:00
12:00
1:00
2:00
3:00
4:00
5:00
6:00
7:00
8:00
9:00
10:00
11:00

Tuesday 9

TODAY'S GOAL

PRIORITIES

1
2
3

5:00
6:00
7:00
8:00
9:00
10:00
11:00
12:00
1:00
2:00
3:00
4:00
5:00
6:00
7:00
8:00
9:00
10:00
11:00

Wednesday 10

TODAY'S GOAL

PRIORITIES

1
2
3

5:00
6:00
7:00
8:00
9:00
10:00
11:00
12:00
1:00
2:00
3:00
4:00
5:00
6:00
7:00
8:00
9:00
10:00
11:00

Thursday 11

Veterans Day

TODAY'S GOAL

PRIORITIES

1
2
3

5:00
6:00
7:00
8:00
9:00
10:00
11:00
12:00
1:00
2:00
3:00
4:00
5:00
6:00
7:00
8:00
9:00
10:00
11:00

Friday 12

TODAY'S GOAL

PRIORITIES

1
2
3

5:00
6:00
7:00
8:00
9:00
10:00
11:00
12:00
1:00
2:00
3:00
4:00
5:00
6:00
7:00
8:00
9:00
10:00
11:00

Saturday 13

TODAY'S GOAL

PRIORITIES

1
2
3

5:00
6:00
7:00
8:00
9:00
10:00
11:00
12:00
1:00
2:00
3:00
4:00
5:00
6:00
7:00
8:00
9:00
10:00
11:00

Sunday 14

TODAY'S GOAL

PRIORITIES

1
2
3

5:00
6:00
7:00
8:00
9:00
10:00
11:00
12:00
1:00
2:00
3:00
4:00
5:00
6:00
7:00
8:00
9:00
10:00
11:00

Gratitude box

November 15-21

This week's priority

Top priority

....
....
....
....

Priority

....
....
....
....

Errands

....
....
....
....

Events ǀ Appointments ǀ Due dates

....
....
....
....
....
....
....
....
....
....

"Keep your mind fixed on what you want in life: not on what you don't want."

– Napoleon Hill

notes ǀ ideas

Positive Habits

	M	T	W	T	F	S	S
Gratitude							
Excercise							
Meditation							
Affirmations							

October

M	T	W	T	F	S	S
				1	2	3
4	5	6	7	8	9	10
11	12	13	14	15	16	17
18	19	20	21	22	23	24
25	26	27	28	29	30	31

November

M	T	W	T	F	S	S
1	2	3	4	5	6	7
8	9	10	11	12	13	14
15	16	17	18	19	20	21
22	23	24	25	26	27	28
29	30					

Monday 15

TODAY'S GOAL

PRIORITIES
1
2
3

5:00	
6:00	
7:00	
8:00	
9:00	
10:00	
11:00	
12:00	
1:00	
2:00	
3:00	
4:00	
5:00	
6:00	
7:00	
8:00	
9:00	
10:00	
11:00	

Tuesday 16

TODAY'S GOAL

PRIORITIES
1
2
3

5:00	
6:00	
7:00	
8:00	
9:00	
10:00	
11:00	
12:00	
1:00	
2:00	
3:00	
4:00	
5:00	
6:00	
7:00	
8:00	
9:00	
10:00	
11:00	

Wednesday 17

TODAY'S GOAL

PRIORITIES
1
2
3

5:00	
6:00	
7:00	
8:00	
9:00	
10:00	
11:00	
12:00	
1:00	
2:00	
3:00	
4:00	
5:00	
6:00	
7:00	
8:00	
9:00	
10:00	
11:00	

Thursday 18

TODAY'S GOAL

PRIORITIES
1
2
3

5:00	
6:00	
7:00	
8:00	
9:00	
10:00	
11:00	
12:00	
1:00	
2:00	
3:00	
4:00	
5:00	
6:00	
7:00	
8:00	
9:00	
10:00	
11:00	

Friday 19

TODAY'S GOAL

PRIORITIES
1
2
3

5:00	
6:00	
7:00	
8:00	
9:00	
10:00	
11:00	
12:00	
1:00	
2:00	
3:00	
4:00	
5:00	
6:00	
7:00	
8:00	
9:00	
10:00	
11:00	

Saturday 20

TODAY'S GOAL

PRIORITIES
1
2
3

5:00	
6:00	
7:00	
8:00	
9:00	
10:00	
11:00	
12:00	
1:00	
2:00	
3:00	
4:00	
5:00	
6:00	
7:00	
8:00	
9:00	
10:00	
11:00	

Sunday 21

TODAY'S GOAL

PRIORITIES
1
2
3

5:00	
6:00	
7:00	
8:00	
9:00	
10:00	
11:00	
12:00	
1:00	
2:00	
3:00	
4:00	
5:00	
6:00	
7:00	
8:00	
9:00	
10:00	
11:00	

Gratitude box

November 22-28

This week's priority

Top priority

....
....
....
....
....

Priority

....
....
....
....

Errands

....
....
....

Events | Appointments | Due dates

....
....
....
....
....
....
....
....
....
....
....

"Everyone visualizes whether he knows it or not.
Visualizing is the great secret of success."

— Genevieve Behrend

notes | ideas

Positive Habits

	M	T	W	T	F	S	S
Gratitude							
Excercise							
Meditation							
Affirmations							

November

M	T	W	T	F	S	S
1	2	3	4	5	6	7
8	9	10	11	12	13	14
15	16	17	18	19	20	21
22	23	24	25	26	27	28
29	30					

December

M	T	W	T	F	S	S
			1	2	3	4
5	6	7	8	9	10	11
12	13	14	15	16	17	18
19	20	21	22	23	24	25
26	27	28	29	30	31	

Monday 22

TODAY'S GOAL

PRIORITIES
1
2
3

5:00
6:00
7:00
8:00
9:00
10:00
11:00
12:00
1:00
2:00
3:00
4:00
5:00
6:00
7:00
8:00
9:00
10:00
11:00

Tuesday 23

TODAY'S GOAL

PRIORITIES
1
2
3

5:00
6:00
7:00
8:00
9:00
10:00
11:00
12:00
1:00
2:00
3:00
4:00
5:00
6:00
7:00
8:00
9:00
10:00
11:00

Wednesday 24

TODAY'S GOAL

PRIORITIES
1
2
3

5:00
6:00
7:00
8:00
9:00
10:00
11:00
12:00
1:00
2:00
3:00
4:00
5:00
6:00
7:00
8:00
9:00
10:00
11:00

Thursday 25

Thanksgiving Day

TODAY'S GOAL

PRIORITIES
1
2
3

5:00
6:00
7:00
8:00
9:00
10:00
11:00
12:00
1:00
2:00
3:00
4:00
5:00
6:00
7:00
8:00
9:00
10:00
11:00

Friday 26

Black Friday

TODAY'S GOAL

PRIORITIES
1
2
3

5:00
6:00
7:00
8:00
9:00
10:00
11:00
12:00
1:00
2:00
3:00
4:00
5:00
6:00
7:00
8:00
9:00
10:00
11:00

Saturday 27

TODAY'S GOAL

PRIORITIES
1
2
3

5:00
6:00
7:00
8:00
9:00
10:00
11:00
12:00
1:00
2:00
3:00
4:00
5:00
6:00
7:00
8:00
9:00
10:00
11:00

Sunday 28

TODAY'S GOAL

PRIORITIES
1
2
3

5:00
6:00
7:00
8:00
9:00
10:00
11:00
12:00
1:00
2:00
3:00
4:00
5:00
6:00
7:00
8:00
9:00
10:00
11:00

Gratitude box

November 29–December 5

This week's priority

Top priority

....
....
....
....
....

Priority

....
....
....
....

Errands

....
....

Events | Appointments | Due dates

....
....
....
....
....
....
....
....
....
....
....
....
....

"To bring anything into your life, imagine that it's already there."

– Richard Bach

notes | ideas

Positive Habits

	M	T	W	T	F	S	S
Gratitude							
Excercise							
Meditation							
Affirmations							

November

M	T	W	T	F	S	S
1	2	3	4	5	6	7
8	9	10	11	12	13	14
15	16	17	18	19	20	21
22	23	24	25	26	27	28
29	30					

December

M	T	W	T	F	S	S
			1	2	3	4
5	6	7	8	9	10	11
12	13	14	15	16	17	18
19	20	21	22	23	24	25
26	27	28	29	30	31	

Monday 29

TODAY'S GOAL

PRIORITIES
1
2
3

5:00	
6:00	
7:00	
8:00	
9:00	
10:00	
11:00	
12:00	
1:00	
2:00	
3:00	
4:00	
5:00	
6:00	
7:00	
8:00	
9:00	
10:00	
11:00	

Tuesday 30

TODAY'S GOAL

PRIORITIES
1
2
3

5:00	
6:00	
7:00	
8:00	
9:00	
10:00	
11:00	
12:00	
1:00	
2:00	
3:00	
4:00	
5:00	
6:00	
7:00	
8:00	
9:00	
10:00	
11:00	

Wednesday 1

TODAY'S GOAL

PRIORITIES
1
2
3

5:00	
6:00	
7:00	
8:00	
9:00	
10:00	
11:00	
12:00	
1:00	
2:00	
3:00	
4:00	
5:00	
6:00	
7:00	
8:00	
9:00	
10:00	
11:00	

Thursday 2

TODAY'S GOAL

PRIORITIES
1
2
3

5:00	
6:00	
7:00	
8:00	
9:00	
10:00	
11:00	
12:00	
1:00	
2:00	
3:00	
4:00	
5:00	
6:00	
7:00	
8:00	
9:00	
10:00	
11:00	

Friday 3

TODAY'S GOAL

PRIORITIES
1
2
3

5:00	
6:00	
7:00	
8:00	
9:00	
10:00	
11:00	
12:00	
1:00	
2:00	
3:00	
4:00	
5:00	
6:00	
7:00	
8:00	
9:00	
10:00	
11:00	

Saturday 4

TODAY'S GOAL

PRIORITIES
1
2
3

5:00	
6:00	
7:00	
8:00	
9:00	
10:00	
11:00	
12:00	
1:00	
2:00	
3:00	
4:00	
5:00	
6:00	
7:00	
8:00	
9:00	
10:00	
11:00	

Sunday 5

TODAY'S GOAL

PRIORITIES
1
2
3

5:00	
6:00	
7:00	
8:00	
9:00	
10:00	
11:00	
12:00	
1:00	
2:00	
3:00	
4:00	
5:00	
6:00	
7:00	
8:00	
9:00	
10:00	
11:00	

Gratitude box

Reflect on your month

When you start actively observing and understanding the invisible parts of yourself – your emotions – you'll equip yourself with the tools to make visible changes in your day-to-day life. Observe how your emotions and feelings change over weeks and months. Become aware of them and change them to more positive feelings so you can attract and manifest the life of your dreams.

Check how balanced you lived your month.

What did I learn this month?

....
....
....
....
....

My top 5 achievements this month

....
....
....
....
....

How was I feeling this month?

Optimistic, Proud, Guilty, Depressed, Peaceful, Lonely, Confused, Disapproval, Happy, Sad, Excited, Disgust, Awful, Surprise, Amazed, Anger, Fear, Disappointed, Insecure, Aggressive, Humiliated, Scared, Hurt, Mad

Did I enjoy what I was doing this month?

....
....
....
....
....

How did I make myself feel good?

....
....
....
....
....

How do I feel about my progress this month?

....
....
....
....
....

What are the greatest insights that I have gained?

....
....
....
....
....

What mental blocks did I encounter?

....
....
....
....
....

What / who inspired me this month?

....
....
....
....
....

What actions can I take to improve?

....
....
....
....
....

December

M	T	W	T	F	S	S
		1	2	3	4	5
6	7	8	9	10	11	12
13	14	15	16	17	18	19
20	21	22	23	24	25	26
27	28	29	30	31		

Monthly
Mood Tracker

Our Mood Tracker is a powerful and easy-to-use tool that allows you to track your emotions – or moods – on a regular basis.

You want to lead a fulfilling, happy life. All of that becomes so much simpler with the Mood Tracker. The perfect mental health support system, this Mood Tracker charts your triggers, looks at your ups and downs, and gives you permission to feel so you can understand your anxiety, support your stress relief, and become happier all around.

By tracking your moods, you may be able to determine situations or times that your mood goes up or down. Such situations are sometimes called triggers. For instance, if you notice you get depressed every time you visit your parents, that's important information that you can use to help you understand yourself better.

Reflect on emotions daily – gain insight into the patterns of your moods, triggers, coping skills, and mindsets.

Chart your emotions. Relieve your anxiety. BUILD A HAPPIER YOU!

COLOR YOUR MOOD

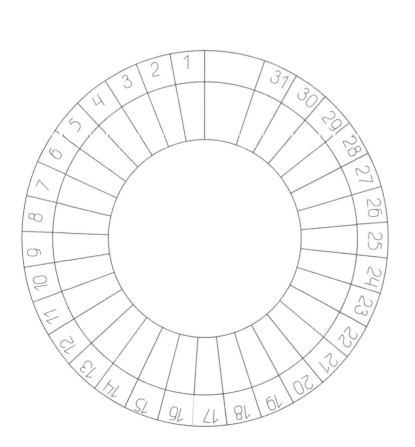

Angry	
Annoyed	
Anxious	
Ashamed	
Confused	
Energetic	
Excited	
Exhausted	
Happy	
Sad	
Relaxed	
Productive	

Monthly Goal Planner

GOAL

REWARD

✓	ACTION STEPS	NOTES

PROGRESS TRACKER

    25%   50%   75%   100%

NOTES

GOAL

REWARD

✓	ACTION STEPS	NOTES

PROGRESS TRACKER

    25%   50%   75%   100%

NOTES

Monthly Habit Tracker

Monthly habit tracker can be particularly powerful on a bad day. When you're feeling down, it's easy to forget about all the progress you have already made. Habit tracking provides visual proof of your hard work – a subtle reminder of how far you've come. Plus, the empty square you see each morning can motivate you to get started because you don't want to lose your progress by breaking your streak.

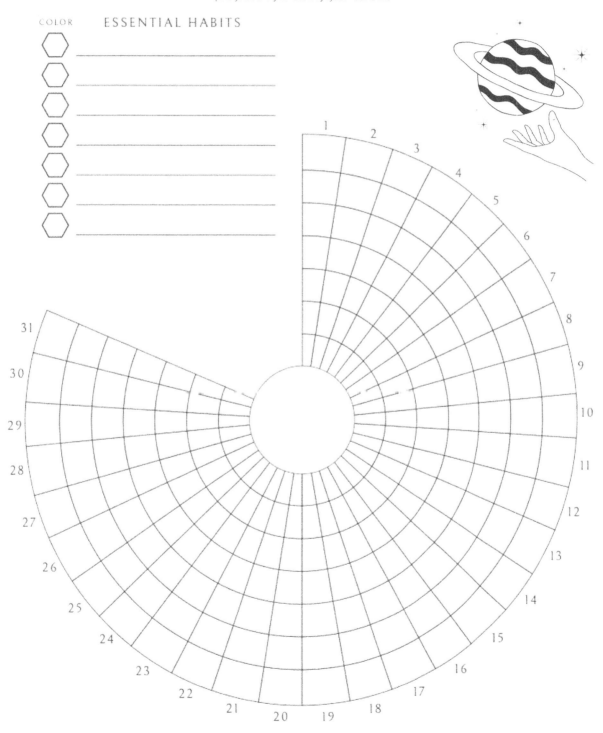

COLOR   ESSENTIAL HABITS

December 6-12

This week's priority

Top priority

....
....
....
....

Priority

....
....
....
....

Errands

....
....
....

Events | Appointments | Due dates

....
....
....
....
....
....
....
....
....
....

"What you radiate outward in your thoughts, feelings, mental pictures and words, you attract into your life."

– Catherine Ponder

notes | ideas

Positive Habits

	M	T	W	T	F	S	S
Gratitude							
Excercise							
Meditation							
Affirmations							

November

M	T	W	T	F	S	S
1	2	3	4	5	6	7
8	9	10	11	12	13	14
15	16	17	18	19	20	21
22	23	24	25	26	27	28
29	30					

December

M	T	W	T	F	S	S
			1	2	3	4
5	6	7	8	9	10	11
12	13	14	15	16	17	18
19	20	21	22	23	24	25
26	27	28	29	30	31	

Monday 6

TODAY'S GOAL

PRIORITIES
1
2
3

5.00	
6.00	
7.00	
8.00	
9.00	
10.00	
11.00	
12.00	
1.00	
2.00	
3.00	
4.00	
5.00	
6.00	
7.00	
8.00	
9.00	
10.00	
11.00	

Tuesday 7

TODAY'S GOAL

PRIORITIES
1
2
3

5.00	
6.00	
7.00	
8.00	
9.00	
10.00	
11.00	
12.00	
1.00	
2.00	
3.00	
4.00	
5.00	
6.00	
7.00	
8.00	
9.00	
10.00	
11.00	

Wednesday 8

TODAY'S GOAL

PRIORITIES
1
2
3

5.00	
6.00	
7.00	
8.00	
9.00	
10.00	
11.00	
12.00	
1.00	
2.00	
3.00	
4.00	
5.00	
6.00	
7.00	
8.00	
9.00	
10.00	
11.00	

Thursday 9

TODAY'S GOAL

PRIORITIES
1
2
3

5.00	
6.00	
7.00	
8.00	
9.00	
10.00	
11.00	
12.00	
1.00	
2.00	
3.00	
4.00	
5.00	
6.00	
7.00	
8.00	
9.00	
10.00	
11.00	

Friday 10

TODAY'S GOAL

PRIORITIES
1
2
3

5.00	
6.00	
7.00	
8.00	
9.00	
10.00	
11.00	
12.00	
1.00	
2.00	
3.00	
4.00	
5.00	
6.00	
7.00	
8.00	
9.00	
10.00	
11.00	

Saturday 11

TODAY'S GOAL

PRIORITIES
1
2
3

5.00	
6.00	
7.00	
8.00	
9.00	
10.00	
11.00	
12.00	
1.00	
2.00	
3.00	
4.00	
5.00	
6.00	
7.00	
8.00	
9.00	
10.00	
11.00	

Sunday 12

TODAY'S GOAL

PRIORITIES
1
2
3

5.00	
6.00	
7.00	
8.00	
9.00	
10.00	
11.00	
12.00	
1.00	
2.00	
3.00	
4.00	
5.00	
6.00	
7.00	
8.00	
9.00	
10.00	
11.00	

Gratitude box

December 13-19

This week's priority

Top priority

....
....
....
....
....

Priority

....
....
....
....

Errands

....
....
....

Events | Appointments | Due dates

....
....
....
....
....
....
....
....
....
....

"It's our intention. Our intention is everything. Nothing happens on this planet without it. Not one single thing has ever been accomplished without intention."

— Jim Carrey

notes | ideas

Positive Habits

	M	T	W	T	F	S	S
Gratitude							
Excercise							
Meditation							
Affirmations							

November

M	T	W	T	F	S	S
1	2	3	4	5	6	7
8	9	10	11	12	13	14
15	16	17	18	19	20	21
22	23	24	25	26	27	28
29	30					

December

M	T	W	T	F	S	S
			1	2	3	4
5	6	7	8	9	10	11
12	13	14	15	16	17	18
19	20	21	22	23	24	25
26	27	28	29	30	31	

Monday 13

TODAY'S GOAL

PRIORITIES

1
2
3

5:00	
6:00	
7:00	
8:00	
9:00	
10:00	
11:00	
12:00	
1:00	
2:00	
3:00	
4:00	
5:00	
6:00	
7:00	
8:00	
9:00	
10:00	
11:00	

Tuesday 14

TODAY'S GOAL

PRIORITIES

1
2
3

5:00	
6:00	
7:00	
8:00	
9:00	
10:00	
11:00	
12:00	
1:00	
2:00	
3:00	
4:00	
5:00	
6:00	
7:00	
8:00	
9:00	
10:00	
11:00	

Wednesday 15

TODAY'S GOAL

PRIORITIES

1
2
3

5:00	
6:00	
7:00	
8:00	
9:00	
10:00	
11:00	
12:00	
1:00	
2:00	
3:00	
4:00	
5:00	
6:00	
7:00	
8:00	
9:00	
10:00	
11:00	

Thursday 16

TODAY'S GOAL

PRIORITIES

1
2
3

5:00	
6:00	
7:00	
8:00	
9:00	
10:00	
11:00	
12:00	
1:00	
2:00	
3:00	
4:00	
5:00	
6:00	
7:00	
8:00	
9:00	
10:00	
11:00	

Friday 17

TODAY'S GOAL

PRIORITIES

1
2
3

5:00	
6:00	
7:00	
8:00	
9:00	
10:00	
11:00	
12:00	
1:00	
2:00	
3:00	
4:00	
5:00	
6:00	
7:00	
8:00	
9:00	
10:00	
11:00	

Saturday 18

TODAY'S GOAL

PRIORITIES

1
2
3

5:00	
6:00	
7:00	
8:00	
9:00	
10:00	
11:00	
12:00	
1:00	
2:00	
3:00	
4:00	
5:00	
6:00	
7:00	
8:00	
9:00	
10:00	
11:00	

Sunday 19

TODAY'S GOAL

PRIORITIES

1
2
3

5:00	
6:00	
7:00	
8:00	
9:00	
10:00	
11:00	
12:00	
1:00	
2:00	
3:00	
4:00	
5:00	
6:00	
7:00	
8:00	
9:00	
10:00	
11:00	

Gratitude box

December 20-26

This week's priority

Top priority

....
....
....
....

Priority

....
....
....
....

Errands

....
....
....

Events | Appointments | Due dates

....
....
....
....
....
....
....
....
....
....

"You are deserving of whatever you want. You truly are. This is one of the most important truths you can come to understand."

– Bob Doyle

notes | ideas

Positive Habits

	M	T	W	T	F	S	S
Gratitude							
Excercise							
Meditation							
Affirmations							

December

M	T	W	T	F	S	S
		1	2	3	4	5
6	7	8	9	10	11	12
13	14	15	16	17	18	19
20	21	22	23	24	25	26
27	28	29	30	31		

January

M	T	W	T	F	S	S
					1	2
3	4	5	6	7	8	9
10	11	12	13	14	15	16
17	18	19	20	21	22	23
24	25	26	27	28	29	30
31						

Monday 20

TODAY'S GOAL

PRIORITIES
1
2
3

5:00	
6:00	
7:00	
8:00	
9:00	
10:00	
11:00	
12:00	
1:00	
2:00	
3:00	
4:00	
5:00	
6:00	
7:00	
8:00	
9:00	
10:00	
11:00	

Tuesday 21

TODAY'S GOAL

PRIORITIES
1
2
3

5:00	
6:00	
7:00	
8:00	
9:00	
10:00	
11:00	
12:00	
1:00	
2:00	
3:00	
4:00	
5:00	
6:00	
7:00	
8:00	
9:00	
10:00	
11:00	

Wednesday 22

TODAY'S GOAL

PRIORITIES
1
2
3

5:00	
6:00	
7:00	
8:00	
9:00	
10:00	
11:00	
12:00	
1:00	
2:00	
3:00	
4:00	
5:00	
6:00	
7:00	
8:00	
9:00	
10:00	
11:00	

Thursday 23

TODAY'S GOAL

PRIORITIES
1
2
3

5:00	
6:00	
7:00	
8:00	
9:00	
10:00	
11:00	
12:00	
1:00	
2:00	
3:00	
4:00	
5:00	
6:00	
7:00	
8:00	
9:00	
10:00	
11:00	

Friday 24

Christmas Eve

TODAY'S GOAL

PRIORITIES
1
2
3

5:00	
6:00	
7:00	
8:00	
9:00	
10:00	
11:00	
12:00	
1:00	
2:00	
3:00	
4:00	
5:00	
6:00	
7:00	
8:00	
9:00	
10:00	
11:00	

Saturday 25

Christmas Day

TODAY'S GOAL

PRIORITIES
1
2
3

5:00	
6:00	
7:00	
8:00	
9:00	
10:00	
11:00	
12:00	
1:00	
2:00	
3:00	
4:00	
5:00	
6:00	
7:00	
8:00	
9:00	
10:00	
11:00	

Sunday 26

TODAY'S GOAL

PRIORITIES
1
2
3

5:00	
6:00	
7:00	
8:00	
9:00	
10:00	
11:00	
12:00	
1:00	
2:00	
3:00	
4:00	
5:00	
6:00	
7:00	
8:00	
9:00	
10:00	
11:00	

Gratitude box

December 27–January 2

This week's priority

Top priority
....
....
....
....
....

Priority
....
....
....
....

Errands
....
....
....

Events | Appointments | Due dates

....
....
....
....
....
....
....
....
....
....

"The only limits in our life are those we impose on ourselves."

– Bob Proctor

notes | ideas

Positive Habits

	M	T	W	T	F	S	S
Gratitude							
Excercise							
Meditation							
Affirmations							

December

M	T	W	T	F	S	S
		1	2	3	4	5
6	7	8	9	10	11	12
13	14	15	16	17	18	19
20	21	22	23	24	25	26
27	28	29	30	31		

January

M	T	W	T	F	S	S
					1	2
3	4	5	6	7	8	9
10	11	12	13	14	15	16
17	18	19	20	21	22	23
24	25	26	27	28	29	30
31						

Monday 27

TODAY'S GOAL

PRIORITIES
1
2
3

5:00
6:00
7:00
8:00
9:00
10:00
11:00
12:00
1:00
2:00
3:00
4:00
5:00
6:00
7:00
8:00
9:00
10:00
11:00

Tuesday 28

TODAY'S GOAL

PRIORITIES
1
2
3

5:00
6:00
7:00
8:00
9:00
10:00
11:00
12:00
1:00
2:00
3:00
4:00
5:00
6:00
7:00
8:00
9:00
10:00
11:00

Wednesday 29

TODAY'S GOAL

PRIORITIES
1
2
3

5:00
6:00
7:00
8:00
9:00
10:00
11:00
12:00
1:00
2:00
3:00
4:00
5:00
6:00
7:00
8:00
9:00
10:00
11:00

Thursday 30

TODAY'S GOAL

PRIORITIES
1
2
3

5:00
6:00
7:00
8:00
9:00
10:00
11:00
12:00
1:00
2:00
3:00
4:00
5:00
6:00
7:00
8:00
9:00
10:00
11:00

Friday 31
New Year's Eve

TODAY'S GOAL

PRIORITIES
1
2
3

5:00
6:00
7:00
8:00
9:00
10:00
11:00
12:00
1:00
2:00
3:00
4:00
5:00
6:00
7:00
8:00
9:00
10:00
11:00

Saturday 1
New Year's Day

TODAY'S GOAL

PRIORITIES
1
2
3

5:00
6:00
7:00
8:00
9:00
10:00
11:00
12:00
1:00
2:00
3:00
4:00
5:00
6:00
7:00
8:00
9:00
10:00
11:00

Sunday 2

TODAY'S GOAL

PRIORITIES
1
2
3

5:00
6:00
7:00
8:00
9:00
10:00
11:00
12:00
1:00
2:00
3:00
4:00
5:00
6:00
7:00
8:00
9:00
10:00
11:00

Gratitude box

Reflect on your month

When you start actively observing and understanding the invisible parts of yourself – your emotions – you'll equip yourself with the tools to make visible changes in your day-to-day life. Observe how your emotions and feelings change over weeks and months. Become aware of them and change them to more positive feelings so you can attract and manifest the life of your dreams.

Check how balanced you lived your month.

What did I learn this month?

....
....
....
....
....

My top 5 achievements this month

....
....
....
....
....

How was I feeling this month?

Optimistic · Proud · Guilty · Depressed · Peaceful · Lonely · Confused · Disapproval · Happy · Sad · Excited · Surprise · Disgust · Awful · Amazed · Fear · Anger · Disappointed · Insecure · Aggressive · Humiliated · Scared · Hurt · Mad

Did I enjoy what I was doing this month?

....
....
....
....
....

How did I make myself feel good?

....
....
....
....
....

How do I feel about my progress this month?

What are the greatest insights that I have gained?

What mental blocks did I encounter?

What / who inspired me this month?

What actions can I take to improve?

Reflect on your year

My TOP 10 achievements this year

_____

_____

_____

_____

_____

_____

_____

What did I learn this year?

_____

_____

_____

_____

What are the greatest insights that I have gained over the past year?

_____

_____

_____

_____

_____

What were the most challenging situations this year? Did I grow from them?

_____

_____

_____

_____

What were my happiest moments this year?

....

....

....

....

What am I most grateful for this year?

....

....

....

....

....

....

....

....

What did I enjoy the most this year?

....

....

....

....

What are my most important goals for next year?

....

....

....

....

....

....

....

....

....

....

Notes

Notes

Notes

Notes

That's all for now!

If you enjoyed this planner, please don't forget to leave a review on Amazon.

Just a simple review helps us a lot!

We create our journals and planners with love and great care, yet mistakes can always happen. For any issues with your planner, such as faulty binding, printing errors, or something else, please do not hesitate to contact us by sending us a DM on Instagram @limitlessabundance_official

Thank you.

Limitless Abundance

 @limitlessabundance_official

Made in the USA
Middletown, DE
02 February 2021